JIMI HENDRIX
SOUNDS AND VISIONS

CONTENTS

INTRODUCTION
page 6

1 ORIGINS
page 12

2 THE TURNING POINT
page 24

3 STARDOM
page 46

4 THE WOMEN IN JIMI'S LIFE
page 116

5 THE GUITAR
page 128

6 THE END
page 160

7 INTERVIEWS
page 184

INTRODUCTION

The 1960s were a decade rich in dynamic personalities. But one personality in particular beautifully encapsulates the most vibrant characteristics of those ten years: Jimi Hendrix. His mad, outlandish, and risky creative instincts helped to impress a kind of manic acceleration upon the world of rock music.

Everything moved quickly during this time. The greatest social changes seemed to be within easy reach—always just around the corner. World events followed one another at a feverish pace. Naturally many people attempted to interpret this collective exhilaration through music.

THE 1960S WERE TEN LONG YEARS OF DREAMS, UTOPIAS, AND ADVENTURES

In just a few short years, Jimi breathed new life into the art of playing the electric guitar and demonstrated how rock music could harness the power of social upheaval.

Nowadays it may be difficult to understand this phenomenon, as everything Jimi invented has been assimilated, digested, and made the new standard. But during the 60s, when the public first witnessed the subversive power of his music, it was a huge shock to the system.

5 *London, 1968: Jimi Hendrix in a photograph for his album* Electric Ladyland

7 *October 1968: Jimi Hendrix performing at the Winterland Ballroom in San Francisco.*

From the first mysterious blues cadenza in "Hey Joe" to the doomsday language in "If 6 Was 9," and from the psychedelic tenderness of "Little Wing" to Jimi's iconic version of the "Star-Spangled Banner" played at Woodstock (the latter of which includes a simulation of bombs being dropped on Vietnam), piece after piece, audiences were spellbound by his exploration of these new frontiers in rock and roll. As is well established, Hendrix exaggerated and consumed everything in his life as though he were in a race against time. This has of course led to his joining the immortal club of those revered but ill-fated artists who helped transform the world from 1960s to the 1970s. Today we might look askance at these excesses of his, which are and will remain an integral part of that period. But there is no doubt that we wouldn't find it hard to choose between the wild and frenzied artistic sensibilities of these heroes and the moderate, big-business ethos that now seems to dominate popular music. Of course we also shouldn't lose ourselves in the romanticism that surrounds this period. In Hendrix's case, he left us with a number of thrilling musical gems that budding guitarists and rock newcomers alike still study and appreciate. And because of his explosive performances and style, he's an easy celebrity to immortalize. A lot of time has passed since the 60s, but in the aftermath, Hendrix's drug use, depression, debt, and fraught personal relationships have become clearer, complicating the mythology of this towering figuring.

Hendrix died 50 years ago. In that time, he has become one of the poster boys of the 1960s, his image solidifying into something grand and immutable. Despite this, Hendrix is actually more alive than ever. His music is still part of the fiery present-day rock scene, and despite the fact that his image is closely linked to such a distinct period, the social consciousness and poeticism of his lyrics seem to have stood the test of time.

All of this is thanks to his incredible talent—that unbelievable mix of rock, soul, funk, avant-garde, noise, passion, and electricity that took him only a handful of years to develop. Therefore, celebrating him today is not just an act of remembrance, or the umpteenth attempt to artificially resurrect the dreams and desires of a decade long buried by commercialism and new technology. Rather, this book is meant to demonstrate that music—free, creative, unbridled music like Jimi Hendrix's—still has a right to exist in this era of manufactured pop hits and streaming. The creative seeds cast by Hendrix half a century ago are still bearing fruit. His story is both beautiful and terrible (and of course the ending is dramatic). But however complicated his legacy may be, one thing is certain—his music lives on.

9 *The Jimi Hendrix Experience in London in the spring of 1967. From left to right: bassist Noel Redding (1945-2003), guitarist Jimi Hendrix (1942-70), and drummer Mitch Mitchell (1947-2008).*

10-11 *This excellent portrait immortalizing Hendrix was taken by Gered Mankowitz in 1967, when the great guitarist's first album* Are You Experienced *had just been released.*

1 ORIGINS

YOUNG JOHNNY ALLEN'S
DIFFICULT CHILDHOOD
BETWEEN LOVE AND ABANDONMENT

Once upon a time, Jimi was Johnny, or, to be more accurate, Johnny Allen Hendrix, born on November 27, 1942. His mother Lucille named him during his birth in Seattle. Jimi's father Al had been drafted into the US Army a few days after their wedding and wasn't present during the birth. In fact, Al's superiors refused to grant him a furlough and kept him imprisoned in the stockade because they were afraid he would go AWOL; he was later sent to the Fiji Islands during the war. Lucille Jeter married Al Hendrix on March 31, 1942, when she was just barely 17 years old. Her young husband had just turned 23. They had met a short time earlier, took to each other immediately, shared a passion for dancing, and were very happy together. But this bright period didn't last. Al was now in the army and Lucille, who was pregnant with Jimi, had to fend for herself. She gave birth to Johnny Hendrix; he weighed about 7 pounds (3.1 kg), had large eyes, a full head of hair, and was one-eighth Cherokee. But due to her young age, her lukewarm attitude toward motherhood, and problems finding work, her life became a constant struggle. She began to drink, moved from one house to another, often had no money or job, and frequently became involved with men who were abusive. Little Johnny was sweet and lovable. Lucille's sister Delores cared for and protected him as much as possible, and she was assisted by her mother Clarice (Jimi's

"I remember my mother held me up to the window. . . . It was fireworks, so it must have been the Fourth of July"

grandmother) and by a family friend named Dorothy Harding. But the situation became increasingly complicated, and Jimi, not even three years old, was sent to California to live with another family, the Champs, who considered adopting him. When Jimi's father returned from the war in November of 1945, he hoped to rebuild his family. He went to California to take his son home and tried to reunite with Lucille. Al had never seen his son, who was now three years old, and had never really lived with Lucille, who in the meantime had become a woman. For a little while everything went smoothly. The young Hendrix family (with their little Johnny) had their "honeymoon" and, despite economic problems, they felt confident their lives would eventually improve. A year after his return, Al decided to baptize his son again, as he didn't care for the names Lucille had given him. Johnny Allen Hendrix officially became James Marshall Hendrix.

In 1946, the Hendrix family finally became a family. But by 1948, storms were brewing again. Lucille didn't care much for the role of mother and wife. She left home often, struggled with alcohol dependency, suffered from depression, which left Al feeling frustrated and angry. The two argued often and broke up and made up again continuously. Little Jimmy suffered greatly because of his parents' tense, often violent relationship. He became withdrawn, spoke little, and couldn't understand the ugly fights that frequently resulted from his parents' heavy drinking. Al moved from job to job, struggling to find a career. The family's constant financial problems sent Lucille further into depression.

In the meantime, young James was growing up. Everyone called him Buster, a nickname given to him by Lucille's sister Delores the night Jimmy was born. She got the name from the famous comic strip character Buster Brown created by cartoonist Richard F. Outcault. Jimmy liked the nickname, partly because he preferred to think that he had been named after Buster Crabbe, the actor who played Flash Gordon in the TV series of the same name, which the boy adored. Flash Gordon was a superhero with supernatural powers who was frequently tasked with saving the world. So to his family and friends, Jimmy was always Buster, a nickname that stuck with him for the rest of his life. Thus it's fair to say he had a sort of second identity. "Jimmy" was a timid, reserved, sensitive boy who occasionally stuttered, while "Buster" was alert, clever, and always bursting with creative ideas.

> "DAD WAS LEVEL-HEADED, MY MOTHER LIKED DRESSING UP. SHE DRANK A LOT BUT WAS GROOVY. THERE WERE ALWAYS PROBLEMS BETWEEN THEM"

Another boy, Leon, was born to the family in 1948, and for a few months during Lucille's pregnancy and after Leon's birth, the atmosphere in the Hendrix family improved. Al was enthusiastic about the arrival of his second son, who soon became his favorite. Eleven months later, in 1949, Lucille gave birth to another boy, Joseph, who unfortunately had serious health issues. The tension between Jimmy's parents increased once again. Al was unable to love the new baby, and the problems of landing a job and providing for the family complicated everything. Jimmy and Leon managed to survive by eating regularly at the homes of neighbors, while little Joe suffered from malnutrition. Given the family's precarious economic situation, Al decided to send the three boys to his mother Nora, who lived in Vancouver, Canada. It was here that Jimmy began attending school. He also learned about his Cherokee roots thanks to his grandmother's descriptions of the family history. A few months later, the three boys returned to their parents in Seattle, where the atmosphere had once again improved. But this period was also short-lived. Jimmy began his second year of school in the autumn of 1950 at the Horace Mann Elementary School in Seattle while living with his

17 *Three year-old James Allen Hendrix photographed with his father, Al Hendrix. His mother Lucille gave birth to him on November 27, 1942.*

Aunt Delores. The usual Hendrix family routine started to resume. Al and Lucille argued constantly. They decided to separate, but then got together again, finding it impossible to live with or without each other.

To further complicate things, the Hendrix family grew with the birth of a daughter, Kathy Ira. She was born blind. She stayed with her family for a little less than a year, after which the family's economic troubles prompted the state of Washington to place her in a foster home. Only a short time later, in October of 1951, another daughter was born: Pamela. Like her siblings Joe and Kathy, she unfortunately suffered from numerous health problems. She too ended up in foster care. As we can imagine, these setbacks and the chaos of the family were a great strain on Jimmy's mental health. On the bright side, he continued to be smothered with affection by his aunts, his grandmother, and Dorothy Harding. He also got along well with his brothers. By the end of 1951, the whole family was briefly reunited, but the situation didn't improve. Lucille's alcoholism was becoming increasingly difficult to manage, and Al's inability to hold down a job meant that there was very little money coming in. Yet the Hendrix family had somehow become accustomed to these difficulties. One of their greatest challenges was little Joe's health. He needed constant medical treatment, which often had to be covered by social health services, as the family usually couldn't afford them. Joe badly needed a leg operation (one of his legs was shorter than the other). However, Al was opposed to the operation, both because he couldn't pay for it and because he didn't feel as though he had any emotional connection to the child. It was then that

Lucille decided to finally leave her husband. They divorced in December of 1951. Formal custody of the children was awarded to Al, but in reality everything remained the same.

In the months that followed, Al and Lucille continued to make up and separate. By the summer of 1952, the situation had reached a breaking point once again. The family decided that the only way to guarantee a future for itself and the necessary medical care for Joe would be to put the boy up for adoption.

Jimmy's life was a free-for-all during this period, but the child who suffered the most from the family's chaotic circumstances was probably Leon, who was often sent to live with a well-to-do family in Seattle while Jimmy got to stay with his father. Throughout all of this, Jimmy attended school, first at the Rainer Vista School, then at Horace Mann, and then at Leschi Elementary School. He became especially close to Leon. In an interview many years later, Leon recalled that the pair lived from hand to mouth, and that, when Jimmy finished school, he would pick Leon up and they would wander around town for hours. Meals usually came from neighbors or family friends. "Jimmy was my whole world, my only friend," Leon stated.

The two tried their best to maintain their relationship with their mother Lucille. She came back home every so often to live with her children and Al for short periods. This ultimately led to the birth of another boy, Alfred, in 1953, who also had congenital physical problems. He was immediately put up for adoption. After the inevitable violent arguments that occurred between Al and Lucille, Lucille would disappear for weeks or months at a time.

Music had not yet burst into little Jimmy's life, but it did make its first appearance. One of his schoolmates, Terry Johnson, attended the nearby Grace Methodist Church, and Jimmy began to go with him. While there, he got his first taste of gospel music. In 1953, he began listening to music on the radio his father had brought home, as by that time Al had secured a steady job. Jimmy began playing the only instrument available: a broomstick. He would dart home from school, turn on the radio, and listen to Perry Como, Frank Sinatra, and Nat King Cole while pretending to play along on his broomstick. Despite all Al's efforts, and despite the constant help offered by Lucille's sister Delores and by Dorothy Harding and her family, Jimmy and Leon lived in difficult conditions and were often left alone.

In 1954, local government agencies decided to intervene, and Al was told that he had to either allow the boys to be fostered or put them up for adoption. He decided that Jimmy, who was 12 at the time, needed less care and could stay at home with him. Leon was sent to a foster home. Fortunately, the family that agreed to take in Leon lived only a few blocks away from the Hendrix home. Thus the two brothers were never really separated. As Leon later stated: "I would go play at our house, or he would come to my place, in fact he often ate with my foster family." But Jimmy was often left alone in the house, with no mother and a barely present father. Now even his youngest brother no longer slept under the same roof. Things only seemed to get worse. Not long after Leon left, Jimmy went to live with his father's cousin Frank for a short period to avoid being fostered.

In 1955, Jimmy enrolled in middle school, first attending Meany Junior High and then Washington Junior High the following year. He was not a particularly good student, but he always managed to pass his classes. He had good relationships with his teachers. Despite being timid, he was well-liked at school and became a Boy Scout. He also tried to play on the Meany Junior High football team, but Jimmy was no athlete. He began to take more of an interest in music. This was partly due to the fact that his father had rented the boys' room in the Hendrix house to Cornell and Ernestine Benson. Ernestine Benson was crazy about blues music.

Thanks to her collection of 78 RPM records, Jimmy became familiar with the music of Howlin' Wolf, Muddy Waters, Robert Johnson, and many of the other leading African American greats. He listened to these legends while playing along on his beloved broomstick. However, in 1956, a real instrument entered his life and transformed it forever—a guitar. There are two versions of this famous occurrence. The more reliable one is an account given by Charles Cross in his book *Room Full of Mirrors*. Jimmy went to live with his father in a boarding house run by the McKay family, whose son owned an old guitar. When the boy decided to stop playing it, Jimmy asked Mrs. McKay if he could have it, and she said she would sell it to him for five dollars. Al certainly did not have the money for a guitar, but for perhaps the first time, Jimmy experienced a bit of luck. Ernestine Benson offered to pay for the guitar, thus giving young Hendrix access to his first real instrument. The second version comes from Jimi himself. It was related in one of the many interviews he gave after he had achieved fame and success. The interview first appeared in the book *Starting at Zero*. "My first instrument was a harmonica, which I got when I was four, I suppose. Next it was a violin. I always dug string instruments and pianos, but I wanted something I could take home or anywhere, and I couldn't take home a piano. Then I started digging guitars. Everybody's house you went into seemed to have one lying around. One night my dad's friend was stoned, and he sold me his guitar for five dollars . . . . I was about 14 or 15 when I started playing guitar. I played in my backyard at home, and kids used to gather 'round and said it was cool."

In 1956, Jimmy fell in love WITH THE GUITAR. His life, and rock music, would never be the same

The guitar was ugly, old, and had only one string, but for Jimmy it was sheer heaven—a sort of spaceship that allowed him to explore unknown worlds. In any case, what was important to Jimmy was that he now had an actual guitar and could go around town with it slung over his shoulder, just like Sterling Hayden in Nicholas Ray's famous movie *Johnny Guitar*. He always kept it by his side, even when he went to bed. His attachment to the instrument only grew after he saw a performance by Elvis Presley in Seattle. He also saw Little Richard and Chuck Berry. Now Jimmy didn't just want to play the guitar—he wanted to play rock and roll. By saving up the money he earned through temporary jobs, he finally managed to buy strings so that he could play his new instrument properly. Although Jimmy was left-handed, he had to learn to play right-handed. As his brother Leon later recalled, their father thought that anything done left-handed was a sign of the devil.

In the meantime, Lucille Jeter, Jimmy's mother, had remarried. Her struggles with alcohol resulted in a number of health problems, and she was now in and out of the hospital. Without telling his father, Jimmy often went to see her. His last visit was in January of 1958. Two weeks later, on February 2, Lucille Jeter, who suffered from cirrhosis of the liver, died of a hemorrhage caused by a ruptured spleen. Jimmy was only 15. Her death was a shattering experience for him. It added to the breakup of the family and the drifting of his siblings. He found consolation in his music. Indeed, music had always been a part of the Hendrix family's life. As mentioned earlier, Al and Lucille were excellent dancers, and in the neighborhood there were always parties that included music. But for Jimmy, listening to music wasn't enough. He wanted to play it and create it. He wanted to be the originator of this extraordinary magic that powered neighborhood parties, church services, and radio broadcasts. For him, music was more than entertainment. Above all, it was a shelter from the tension, chaos, and pain of everyday life. He played the guitar for hours and hours each day, listened to all kinds of music, and took a special interest in blues and rock and roll.

Through music, he had a means to harmonize with the parts of his nature that had remained hidden until now. His guitar was more than an instrument—it was the key to becoming somebody in the world. He convinced his father that he really needed an electric guitar, and Al, spurred on by Ernestine Benson—who in the meantime had reunited with her husband and had resumed living in the Hendrix home—realized that music was the only way he could have a positive relationship with his timid and introverted son. He decided to purchase an electric guitar for Jimmy. Jimmy never took music lessons. Instead, he listened to everything he could: Ernestine Benson's records, the shows and live performances held throughout Seattle, and the music played by his friends. The guitar, which was already a dear friend during this time, became the center of his universe. But now that he finally had an electric guitar, Jimmy needed to find a band.

In 1959, he enrolled in Garfield High School in the Central District of Seattle, but academics no longer interested Jimmy. School had nothing to offer him except opportunities to meet friends and become a member of a band. The first band he played with was called The Velvetones. The band performed rock and roll songs in the Seattle area, playing house shows and other small venues.

Jimmy played the guitar solos. Sometimes he played the bass using the lower strings of his guitar. Every so often he also played rhythm. At night, he went out often, listening to every band that played in the area and learning from them all. He copied whatever interested him, improved on it, and made it his very own. He played with bands such as The Rocking Kings, which allowed him to play most of their guitar solos and even to sing, and The Tomcats. He jammed with anyone who happened to be interested and constantly improved his technique and style. At the same time, he began developing a stage presence and attitude, practicing routines such as playing the guitar behind his head. For a brief period, he quit going to school. He enrolled again at Garfield High School the following year, but a short time later, in October of 1960, he abandoned his studies for good and began to work with his father. But his true passion was obviously music. For the most part, he kept out of trouble. However, on May 2, 1961, he was arrested for joyriding. Three days later he did it again. In both cases, young Jimmy explained that he didn't realize the cars were stolen. During the first arrest, he spent only one night in jail. But during the second arrest, he was imprisoned for a whole week. Two arrests meant a criminal trial and possibly more jail time. He won a two-year suspended sentence provided he agree to join the US Army.

"I DIDN'T HAVE A CENT IN MY POCKET. SO I WALKED INTO THE FIRST OFFICE I SAW AND VOLUNTEERED"

In 1961, after eight weeks of basic training at Fort Ord in California, Jimmy became a paratrooper in the 101st Airborne Division.

He was stationed at Fort Campbell in Kentucky and believed he might become a career military man. Flying in planes and jumping out of them were tremendously satisfying experiences, as he wrote in a letter to his father. He stated that parachute jumps "were the most thrilling thing he had ever done." He said much the same thing years later during an interview for the New Musical Express: "It's the most alone feeling the world. You're there all by yourself . . . then you feel a tug on your collar and you're supposed to look up to see if your chute is open. And so you look up, and there's that big, beautiful white mushroom above you. And at this point you begin talking to yourself." What is most incredible is that Jimmy did not take along his guitar during this pivotal phase in his life. It was almost as if Jimmy had decided to put his dreams to the test. He hoped to try something new and see if a career outside of music were really possible. Three months later, on January 17, 1962, he brought this strange period to an end. Everything became clear to him. He wrote another letter to his father, this time asking him to send his guitar "as soon as possible, I really need it now." The guitar, a red Danelectro U-1, arrived at Fort Campbell a few weeks later. Jimmy and his guitar never separated again.

With Billy Cox, he played his first professional gig and earned 35 cents and three hamburgers

Jimmy's time in the military was lonely. He missed his friends while in his barracks and felt as though he had nobody with him to share in the excitement of the flights and parachute jumps he completed. Above all, Jimmy noticed his life was lacking without music. He resumed playing the guitar obsessively, holing up in his room in the barracks. His fellow soldiers considered him something of a loner. He never "let his hair down," which would have been typical hippie behavior, but he didn't associate much with the other soldiers, preferring the company of his beloved red Danelectro.

One evening, while he was playing in one of the large rooms in the barracks, a young serviceman named Billy Cox, newly arrived from Wheeling, Virginia, heard the sound of Jimmy's guitar while passing by a window. He entered the room and introduced himself to Hendrix, telling him that he, too, was in love with music, especially with the blues, and that he played the bass guitar. Cox was a few years older than Hendrix and had a bit more musical experience. He had also studied music in Pittsburgh, where he had grown up. The two got along well and decided to form a band together. They became friends and remained so until Hendrix's death.

Jimmy and Cox followed through with their plan. The band didn't have an official name, and its other members came and went. But they played every week in clubs near the fort. "I remember my first gig was at an armory, a National Guard place," Hendrix recalled in *Starting at Zero*, "and we earned 35 cents apiece and three hamburgers. It was so hard for me at first. I knew about three songs, and when it was time for us to play onstage I was all shaky, so I had to play behind the curtains. And then you get so very discouraged. You hear different bands playing around you and the guitar player always seems like he's so much better than you are. Most people give up at this point, but it's best not to. Just keep on, just keep on."

Gradually, music and the band became all that mattered to Jimmy. The two friends finally hit upon a name for the band: The King Kasuals. They began playing gigs in towns outside the fort. Fort Campbell was about 60 miles (96 km) from Nashville, so many of their early shows took place there. Cox was about to finish his military service, but Jimmy still had another two years. The only solution was to force Uncle Sam to send him home. For several weeks, he pretended to be sick, slept while on duty, and displayed many strange habits and tics, demonstrating that he wasn't suited for a military career. Eventually he got a discharge. Now Jimmy was free to develop his band with Cox.

Now there was no obstacle between him and music.

2 THE TURNING POINT

COMBINING SOUL, FUNK, AND BLUES, JIMI TURNED HIS DREAMS INTO REALITY

Instead of going back to Seattle, Jimmy went to Clarksville, Tennessee, where he waited for Billy Cox to finish his military service. There Jimmy began a penniless, bohemian life filled with music. From late 1962 to early 1963, Hendrix earned a precarious living by playing his guitar in the Nashville area. The King Kasuals played in clubs and bars. Jimmy also played as a backing musician for other bands or at very small gigs with Cox. His pay was usually only a few dollars and a meal or two, but he played and practiced continuously, determined to become a great guitarist. His guitar was his faithful companion, the spyglass through which he caught glimpses of his bright future. In no time at all, his skills increased exponentially and his style became more and more polished and unique. And his musical career wasn't just limited to practicing. He also went to the performances of any guitarist who happened

ONSTAGE, HE BECAME A DIFFERENT PERSON, USING EVERY TRICK IN THE BOOK

to wind up in Nashville. He learned a great deal from Johnny Jones, the solo guitarist of the band The Imperials, who introduced him to other greats like B.B. King and Albert King. This period was a whirlwind for Hendrix. At this time most of his money came from working as a hired or backing musician. He played in the bars and clubs that made up the so-called "Chitlin' Circuit," a collection of venues in which African American musicians and other entertainers could perform to audiences that were prevalently black in the Deep South, where segregation was still a big part of everyday life. These experiences served as an excellent apprenticeship for Hendrix. He learned about stage presence and how to entertain audiences and keep their attention while at the same time playing in many different styles. He learned how to play the guitar behind his back like T-Bone Walker and how to play it with his teeth like Alphonso Young. He had an unusually long cord connecting his guitar to his amplifier, and this allowed him the freedom of movement to engage the audience and impress them with his guitar tricks. "Some cat tried to get me to play behind my head because I would never move too much," he states in *Starting at Zero*. "I said, 'Oh man, who wants to do all that junk?' But when you play in front a public that is never satisfied, sooner or later you begin to think you are boring. The idea of playing with my teeth came to me in a town in Tennessee. Down there you have to play with your teeth or else you get shot. There's a trail of broken teeth all over the stage. When you play with your teeth you have to know what you're doing or you might hurt yourself. A lot of people think that what I do with guitar is vulgar. I don't agree. It might be erotic, but what music with rhythm isn't? Music is such an intimate form of expression that it can't help evoking sex. So what's wrong with that? Is it really so obscene? More obscene than any erotic publicity you see in the newspapers or on TV?"

Jimmy was gifted and, unlike many of his fellow musicians, he didn't need to have another job to support himself, as he always had plenty of offers to play in small gigs. He played with Carla Thomas, Jerry Butler, and Slim Harpo. He went on a short tour with Solomon Burke's band, along with Joe Tex and Otis Redding. Burke couldn't tolerate Jimmy's wild personality and style and his disregard for the rules. Thus he decided to "bequeath" him to Otis Redding's band. But even there Jimmy didn't seem to fit in. He passed on an offer to join The Marvelettes on tour with Curtis Mayfield. He played with Bobby Womack and then with Gorgeous George Odell, and became part of the backing bands supporting Sam Cooke, Jackie Wilson, and Little Richard. In December of 1963, he accepted a promoter's offer to go to New York. All at once he abandoned The King Kasuals and the South.

He arrived in the Big Apple in January of 1964. He was twenty years old. At first things were worse than before, as it was extremely difficult to enter the circuit of New York nightclub musicians. But a month later, Jimmy seized an opportunity: The Isley Brothers were looking for a new guitarist and let him join the band. In March, he went to a recording studio for the first time to record the song "Testify" with the band. His experience with The Isley Brothers took him to a different level professionally, both in terms of his live performances and his skills in the recording studio. This was one of the most successful rhythm and blues bands in the United States, and Jimmy had become part of the "big league." However, here the rules were very different. Musicians had to dress a certain way, maintain certain hairstyles, and move on stage according to predetermined routines. If these rules weren't respected, band promoters could withhold pay. This was certainly not Jimmy's way of doing things. Consequently, he eventually left The Isley Brothers and went to Memphis, Kansas City, and Atlanta. It was in the Georgia capital that he became friends with one of the members of Little Richard's band. When he saw Jimmy's guitar skills, he asked him if he wanted to audition to join the group.

28 *The Isley Brothers playing at a party for the DJ Nathaniel "Magnificent" Montague at the Armory in Harlem, New York City (1964). Jimi Hendrix is on the far left, playing the guitar.*

29 *Curtis Knight and The Squires in 1966. From left to right: Jimi Hendrix, an unidentified musician, Curtis Knight, Lonnie Youngblood, and Ace Halls.*

So Jimmy found himself playing with a legend that he had seen perform in Seattle back when he was a kid. Jimmy even performed on television for the first time, in June of 1965 in Nashville. Even though Little Richard's band was probably one of the best in the United States at this time as far as technique and sound are concerned, playing for others felt like being in a straightjacket. Jimmy could hardly bear the rules that Little Richard imposed on his backing musicians. Hendrix wanted to innovate and try new things. In short, he wanted to break free and fly solo.

He left Little Richard's band and resumed his previous life in Harlem. Once again he was penniless, jamming with other musicians and recording singles written by others. In the summer of 1965, he wrote a letter to his father: "When you're playing behind other people you're still not making a name for yourself as you would if you were working for yourself.... So just in case about three or four months from now you might hear a record by me which sounds terrible, don't feel ashamed, just wait until the money rolls in because every day people are singing worse and worse on purpose and the public buys more and more records." He signed the letter "Maurice James," but he had already begun calling himself Jimmy James or Jimmy Jim. He was on the hunt for a pseudonym, just as he was searching for a unique sound. Jimmy imagined a future completely different from the turbulent past he had experienced. He loved to change things, could never stay still, had no routines or habits, and was always searching for something new in both life and art. In October of 1965, he met Curtis Knight and became a member of his Squires band. This group wasn't as professional as many of the others Jimmy had played with,

but it had one important advantage for him: he was the main attraction and was given much more freedom in terms of his music and stage antics. Knight's producer was Ed Chalpin, who immediately noticed Hendrix's gifts and offered him a contract that same month. Jimmy recorded at least 30 songs for Chalpin and Knight (including one featuring Jane Mansfield). The quality of the music was obviously important to Jimmy, but he was also interested in the inner workings of recording studios. He wanted to know the techniques employed to achieve certain sounds so that he could master them and improve upon them in the future. But overall this was a rough patch in Jimmy's career. He felt hopeless and alone. Despite New York's size, it didn't seem to offer him much more than the other cities he had worked in. It was still difficult to earn a living and keep food on the table.

Jimmy had not yet become Jimi. Earlier pseudonyms included: Maurice James, Jimmy James, and Jimmy Jim.

When 1966 arrived, he celebrated his 23rd birthday, but the future didn't look bright. He began playing with Joey Dee and The Starliters, and then with King Curtis. He recorded plenty of music, but nothing seemed to change. He came to the conclusion that it was time to leave Harlem and the African American music circuit. Music was changing, and Jimmy could feel it. Rock was becoming the dominant form of popular music, and the Beatles had just invaded the United States along with a host of other English rock bands. Bob Dylan arrived on the scene. Young people started rebelling against their parents and letting their hair grow long. The world was changing quickly, and this new world was the one Jimmy wanted to live in. He had already begun writing his own songs. He noticed that nothing he wrote sounded like the soul or blues he had to play in nightclubs to earn a living. Bob Dylan became a source of inspiration for Jimmy, and his songs began to sound more and more like hard rock.

The Beatles arrived.
YOUNG PEOPLE CHANGED
almost overnight, rebelling against everything

Life plodded on. Hendrix played wherever he could and tried to meet new people, particularly young women. His penchant for one-night stands is of course well-documented. One important acquaintance was Linda Keith, a 20-year-old English model. She was the perfect example of a swinging London girl and happened to be the fiancée of Rolling Stones guitarist Keith Richards. Hendrix met her at the Cheetah Club during his last performance with King Curtis and The Squires. Linda watched him and listened to him, became curious, and after the concert she and her English friends invited Jimmy back to their apartment. Here Hendrix had his first experience with LSD, which at the time was still legal.

30 *Hendrix poses for a portrait. At this time he had just had his first forays into the psychedelic world and LSD, which remained important for him for the rest of his life.*

Jimmy had made his entrance into the psychedelic world, which in many respects he would never abandon. Acid became a new way of looking at things—one that seemed to fit his creative tastes. His songs weren't necessarily the results of LSD-enduced visions, but these visions certainly helped him achieve the mindset he wanted as he got to work writing his own music.

Two weeks after that meeting, another important one took place. Once again it was at the Cheetah Club in New York. Jimmy met Richie Havens, who had been thunderstruck by his guitar playing and suggested that the ideal place for Jimmy and his music would be Greenwich Village, where "everything was happening." Havens also advised him to go to one of the leading clubs on the music scene, the Cafè Wha?. After a brief audition there, Jimmy was guaranteed a series of evening shows. Now he just needed a few backing musicians. On the streets of New York, he found Randy Wolfe, a 15-year-old who had run away from home (and who would go on to become the rock star Randy California with the band Spirit), and Jeff "Skunk" Baxter (a future legendary session man and member of the Doobie Brothers band). The three chose a simple name for their new band: Jimmy James and The Blue Flames. After a few concerts, Jimmy decided to change his name to Jimi, which sounded more exotic and mysterious. Unfortunately for Jimi, his new band had a high turnover of backing musicians. The band played paid gigs for the most part, but their covers of established songs always deviated from the originals. Jimi could finally play the kinds of songs he wanted, including Howlin' Wolf's "Killing Floor," Dylan's "Like a Rolling Stone," and "Wild Thing" by The Troggs.

THE CLUBS AND BARS OF GREENWICH VILLAGE WERE PERFECT FOR JIMI

But Jimi's approach to these songs was completely his own. He experimented with fuzz and distortion effects to achieve a heavier sound. One of the members of the band The Fugs made him a primitive fuzz pedal. This changed everything: now he had his own unique sound. And now he could freely play the guitar behind his back, with his teeth, or between his legs—tricks the audiences of white youngsters in Greenwich Village had never seen before. At this point, Jimi was earning about ten dollars a performance. This still wasn't much, but it was far more than he had ever earned in his life.

32 *The English model Linda Keith, who was first the girlfriend of Keith Richards of the Rolling Stones. She also had a relationship with Jimi Hendrix.*

He was no longer James Marshall Hendrix, or Jimmy, or even little Buster. He had finally become who he was always meant to be: Jimi Hendrix.

At the Café Wha?, Jimi began to develop a small following of dedicated fans, but his real supporters were other musicians, such as Mike Bloomfield. Thanks to the recommendations of Richie Havens, Linda Keith, Andrew Loog Oldham (the producer of the Rolling Stones), and Seymour Stein (the boss of Sire Records), Jimi's career slowly began to take off. Linda even managed to bring the Stones themselves to a Blue Flames concert at the Ondine Disco in New York. Despite their admiration for Hendrix and his performances, they still did not ask him to join their band. But things began to change when Chas Chandler, the bassist of the band The Animals, went to hear him play. The Animals were one of the most popular bands in both the UK and the US, but Chandler had decided to leave the group at the end of their 1966 American tour. He wanted to become a record producer. On August 2, Linda Keith suggested he go with her to hear and meet Jimi Hendrix. So the following evening, Chandler went to the Café Wha?, saw Jimi perform, and was stunned: "I thought immediately that he was the best guitarist I'd ever seen."

During the "British Invasion," many English musicians went to the United States to seek their fortunes.

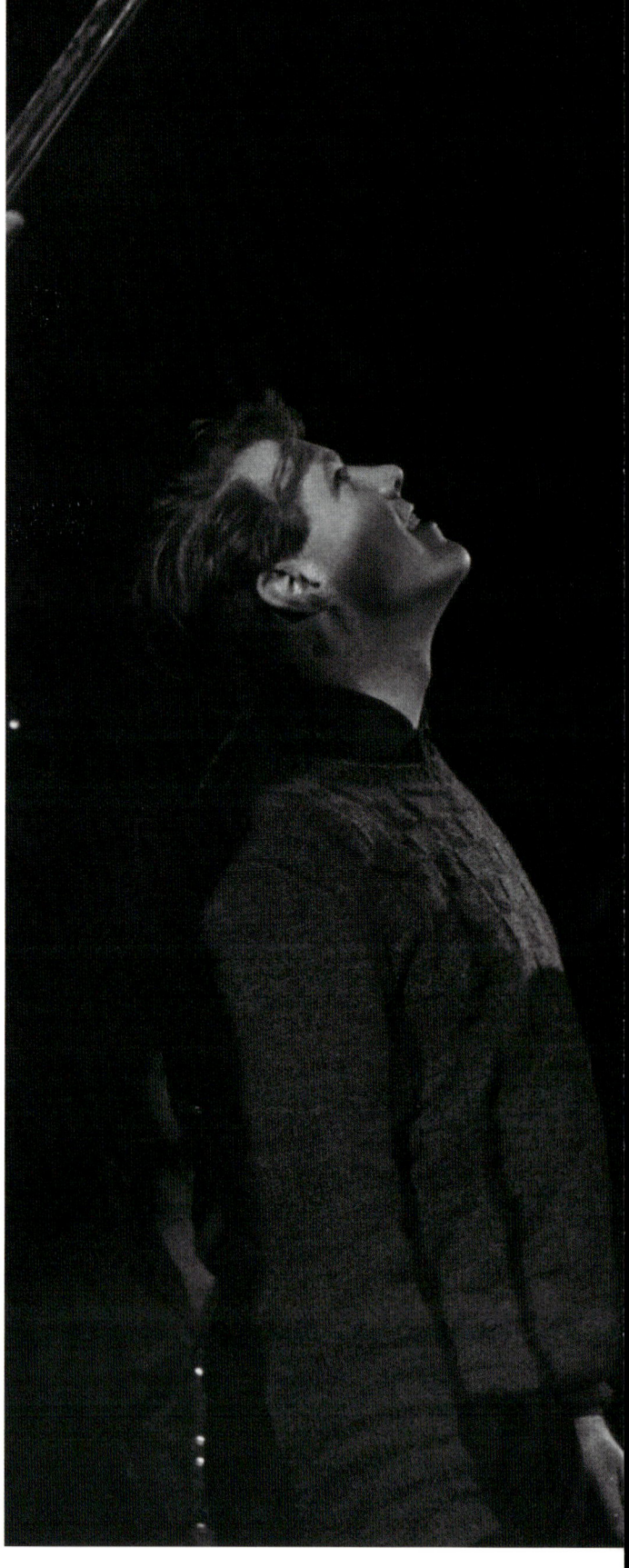

34-35 *The English musician Chas Chandler, formerly a member of the band The Animals, speaking onstage with Jimi Hendrix. Chandler became Jimi's producer.*

36 *The bassist Noel Redding performing at the Star Club in Hamburg, Germany. At this time he was not yet a member of the Experience.*

37 *Drummer Mitch Mitchell during a performance.*

It was Hendrix's version of "Hey Joe," a song by Tim Rose, that impressed Chandler the most, as he had always liked the song. He wondered if he might be able to introduce the song to England. Chas and Hendrix decided immediately that they would work together, and Chandler proposed taking the young guitarist with him back to England. After Chandler finished up his last tour with The Animals a month later, the two were ready to leave. Jimi and his co-managers Chas Chandler and Michael Jeffrey left on the evening of September 23, 1966.

In 1966, London was the center of the world in terms of art, music, fashion, and literature. Youth culture was undergoing a transformation. A sound and color revolution was in progress, and everybody's hair grew longer as their skirts got shorter. It was a great time to be young, and London was the perfect place for anyone angling to change their lives in a big way. The Beatles now presided over an exploding rock scene, and every bar and club in London was featuring rock musicians in some capacity. London was the capital of a new sound that had overwhelmed music charts around the world. Chandler immediately got to work forming a band for Hendrix. His first selection was Noel Redding, a young guitarist who had responded to an ad Chandler had run in the magazine *Melody Maker*. After a jam session with Jimi, he was recruited as the group's bassist.

There are many legends about Hendrix's first week in London. Almost all of them are false, but a few are true, like the one about Jimi's sixth day in the English capital. In New York, Chandler had promised Jimi a meeting with Eric Clapton, who at the time was a member of the band Cream. Clapton was considered an electric guitar god at the time. Chandler did indeed secure the meeting. It took place at Central London Polytechnic, where Cream was playing a concert. Chandler asked the Cream members if Jimi could go onstage and jam with them. They agreed, and Jimi plugged his guitar into Jack Bruce's amplifier.

They played an extremely fast version of the song "Killing Floor." Clapton was stunned by Hendrix's power and creativity, and the same went for Jeff Beck of the band The Yardbirds, who happened to be in the audience.

Just a few days later, Jimi met "the French Presley," a rocker by the name of Johnny Halliday, who had heard him play in a club and offered to let him play as his opening act on a two-week tour of France. Hendrix agreed, but he and Redding didn't have a drummer yet, so they recruited 20-year-old Mitch Mitchell, who had just left Georgie Fame's band. With this lineup in place, The Jimi Hendrix Experience was born.

38-39 The Jimi Hendrix Experience soon conquered the London public with its vibrant shows. Here they can be seen posing backstage at the Saville Theatre in January of 1967. From left to right: Noel Redding, Jimi Hendrix, and Mitch Mitchell.

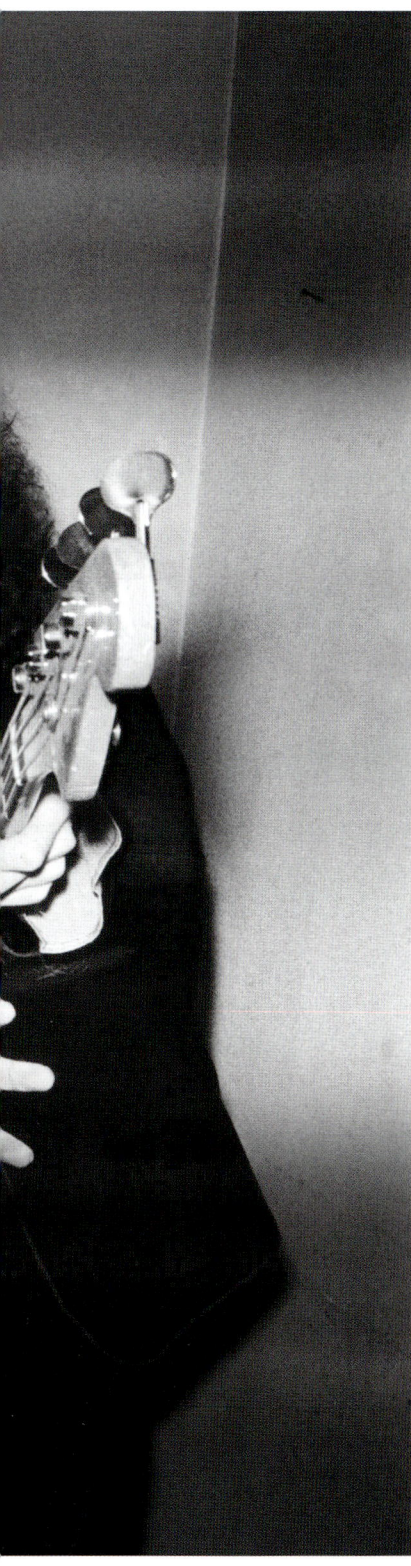

For many English rockers, blues music was the key to opening up a new frontier in music

40-41 *Hendrix became the darling of the British rock scene. This photograph shows Hendrix together with Eric Burdon, the lead singer of The Animals, and bassist Noel Redding.*

41 *Another photograph of the Experience: Mitch Mitchell, Jimi Hendrix, and Noel Redding drinking tea backstage.*

1967

44-45 A powerful image of the famous trio from 1968, with Hendrix in the middle. From left to right: Noel Redding, Jimi Hendrix, and Mitch Mitchell.

3 STARDOM

JIMI AND HIS GUITAR LEFT LONDON TO CONQUER THE WORLD

When he returned from France (exactly one month after his arrival in England), Hendrix went to the recording studio with his new band to record their first single, "Hey Joe." The trio began playing shows in small London clubs, such as Bag O' Nails, Scotch of St. James, Blaises, Speakeasy, Ram Jam Club, and The Upper Cut. Their audiences began to grow in size. Every musician in town wanted to hear Jimi play, and they always left impressed with the guitar skills of this singular young American. After receiving rejections from Decca and other big record labels, Chandler succeeded in convincing Chris Stamp and Kit Lambert—managers of the band The Who who also ran a label called Track Records—to release "Hey Joe." He also arranged to have Jimi Hendrix and the Experience appear on *Ready Steady Go*, one of the most popular television musical

THE ROYAL FAMILY OF ENGLISH ROCK
BOWED DOWN BEFORE
their new electric guitar king

programs in existence, to play their new single on the day of its release, on December 16, 1966. "Hey Joe" was an immediate hit, peaking at number four on the United Kingdom Singles Chart.

The year 1967 began with a bang. Hendrix and his band were on the radio and on television. With the support of Mitchell and Redding, Hendrix grew substantially as a songwriter and musician. The band set to work on their first album, *Are You Experienced*, which they began recording at De Lane Lea Studios in the heart of Soho. Additional recordings were made at CBS Studios and at the glorious Olympic Studios in London.

In the meantime, Hendrix, Redding, and Mitchell continued to perform at a wild pace. They would go to nearby cities for concerts, play, and then immediately return to London to continue recording in the middle of the night. And when they weren't playing out of town, they naturally had gigs in London. On the evening of January 11, 1967, after spending about four hours working on the recording of the song "Purple Haze," the band went to perform live at the Bag O'Nails, a small club in Soho. Here the audience included personalities such as Eric Clapton, Jeff Beck, Jimmy Page, Paul McCartney, Ringo Starr, John Lennon, Beatles manager Brian Epstein, Pete Townshend, John Entwistle, Mick Jagger, Brian Jones, Donovan, Georgie Fame, Denny Laine, as well as all the members of the three bands The Hollies, The Small Faces, and The Animals. In other words, the cream of British rock had come to pay homage to the new prophet of the electric guitar. Hendrix played like no other guitarist in existence. His music was a signature blend of soul, rhythm and blues, rock, and psychedelia. His nimble fingers conjured up songs about the difficulties of relationships and commitments. It was music that exuded sex and spirituality and that seemed as ethereal and abstract as it did earthly.

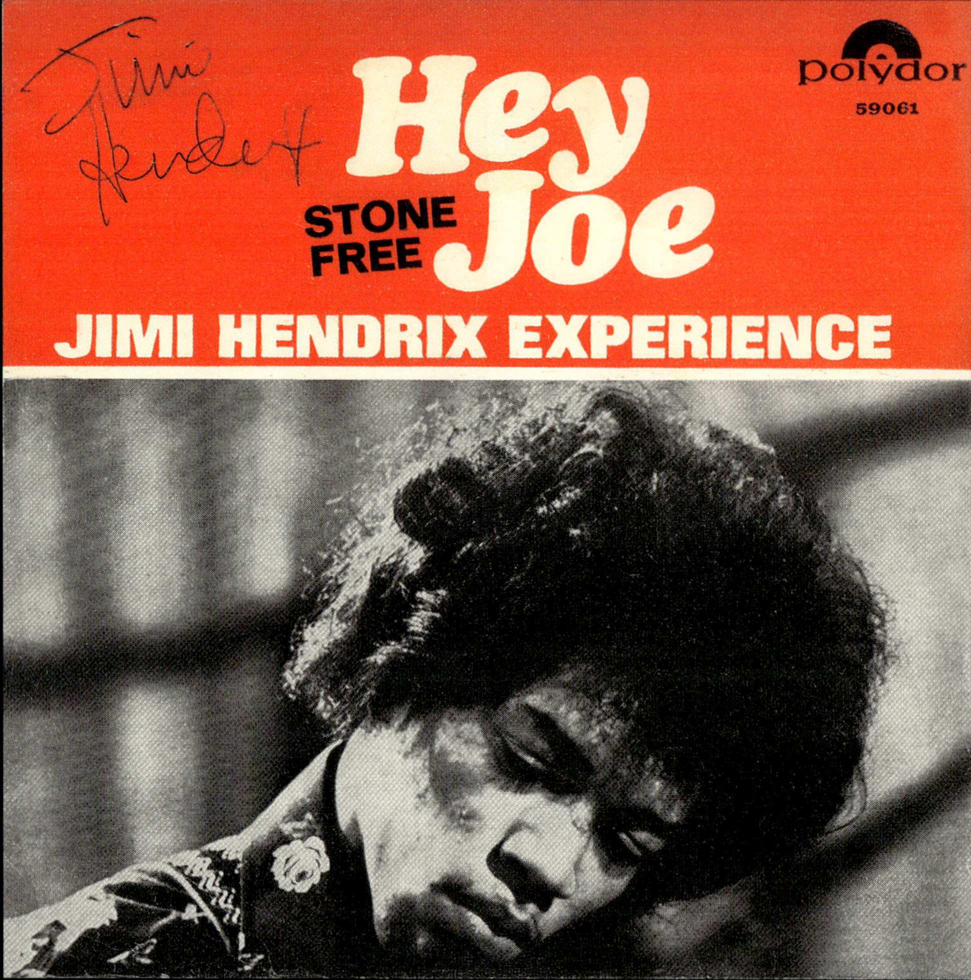
polydor
59061
Hey Joe
STONE FREE
JIMI HENDRIX EXPERIENCE

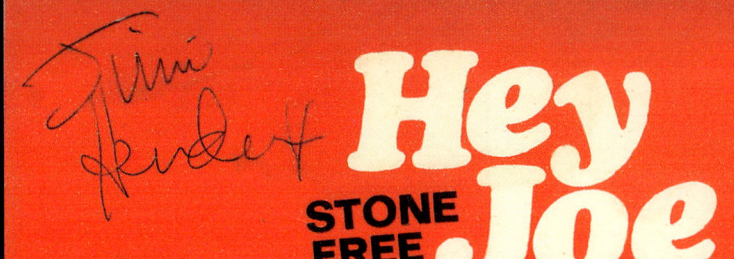

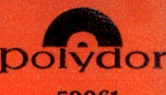

1967

Are You Experienced was completed in the spring of 1967, five months after the band had begun recording it. In total, they had spent only 72 hours in the recording studio. When it was released, it immediately went to the top of the charts, peaking at number two. The Beatles' *Sgt. Pepper's Lonely Hearts Club Band* occupied the number one spot. The album was simply overwhelming. It had echoes of Dylan, Clapton, and James Brown, as the promotional blurbs announced, but it was much more than that. Above all, the electric guitar played a much larger role than it had on the albums of Jimi's influences. It had become the principal instrument of the rock revolution, and bands like The Beatles and The Rolling Stones were taking blues songs and giving them more of an edge with sounds that could only be produced on the electric guitar. But for Hendrix, the electric

The Jimi Hendrix Experience USHERED IN ROCK'S psychedelic period

guitar seemed more like a full orchestra than a single instrument. Sure you could just play notes and chords, but Jimi was at the forefront of distortion, fuzz, and other guitar effects. With the help of technician Roger Mayer, noises, echoes, reverberations, whistles, and hisses made it onto the band's studio recordings. Interestingly, the album was mostly recorded live, with Hendrix playing full blast. Unknown to the band, Chandler had taped many rehearsals in order to save time and money. Sound engineer Eddie Kramer, who worked with Hendrix on most of his recordings, helped the band achieve the unique sound it was looking for during the production process.

---

52 *The cover of The Jimi Hendrix Experience's debut album,* Are You Experienced, *released in England in May of 1967 by Track Records. The photograph was taken by Bruce Fleming.*

54 *Jimi Hendrix during a performance at the Ahoy Club in Rotterdam, Netherlands (December 1, 1967). The American guitarist had become an international success.*

55 *Another photograph of the same 1967 performance, which was televised. Jimi is in the foreground, accompanied by Noel Redding.*

Jimi had changed in only a few weeks. He had attained a new level of consciousness, a major confidence boost, and more faith in his own abilities: "I believe in myself more than anything," he said in an interview published in *Starting at Zero*. "I suppose, in a way, that's also believing in God. If there is a God and He made you, then if you believe in yourself you're also believing in Him. So I think everybody should believe in himself. That doesn't mean you've got to believe in heaven and hell and all that stuff. But it does mean that what you are and what you do is your religion. . . .When I get up on stage—well, that's my whole life. *That's* my religion. My music is electric church music, if by 'church' you mean 'religion.' I am electric religion."

Jimi entered the recording studio, and in just a short time, he created an explosion of sounds and colors

Are You Experienced contains 11 songs in total, from "Foxy Lady," which opens the album with a guitar explosion that leaves no doubt that listeners are about to enter a new world of sound—to "Are You Experienced," which concludes with a simple request: leave the old world behind and try out the new one. Abandon old routines and patterns and experiment with fresh ones. In short, open your mind to the "experience." The song may have capped the album, but it initiated the listener into a brand-new scene. Other exellent tracks include "Manic Depression," which highlights Mitch Mitchell's drumming expertise, "Red House," which mixes blues wth Jimi's wild soloing abilities,

"I Don't Live Today," which was one of the first recorded songs to utilize the wah-wah effect and which also alludes to the Cherokee roots of Jimi's paternal grandmother Nora, the ballad "May This Be Love," which reveals the gentler side of Jimi's talents, the staggering track "Fire," which is a psychedelic journey packed into three minutes, and "Third Stone From the Sun," in which experimentatal sounds are merged with hard-rocking drums.

As is deteailed in Chas Chandler's memoirs and in the accounts of many other musicians and technicians working during this time, Hendrix's first singles and album were masterpieces of improvisation, as much of this material had come together only during the months leading up to the recording process. Up until then, he had always played covers of songs written by other people, with bands in which he was either a backing musician or one of several guitarists. On top of this, Hendrix didn't need many takes—he frequently nailed recordings on the first try. Mitchell and Redding often had to learn Jimi's songs on the fly in the recording studio, as they usually hadn't heard them before. The trio played exceptionally well together, which was extraordinary given that they barely knew each other. They were quite different from the typical blues or rock trio and managed to work many different sounds into their recordings—often at the last moment and adhering only to their own instincts. Sound engineer Ed Kramer's arrival and the move to Olympic Studios in London for recording took the band to a new level, as Kramer introduced many innovative techniques and effects, taking full advantage of the possibilities afforded by four-track recording, thus giving Hendrix more creative freedom.

March 1, 1967 marked the release of the Experience's second single, "Purple Haze," written by Hendrix. It's an explosive work that reached the number three spot on the charts. It was the band's most psychedelic song yet, and one of the tracks that really helped to differentiate them from the other rock bands working in the UK and the US. The following week, the band continued working on the album *Are You Experienced*, which they completed on April 25. That same day, Chas Chandler brought a demo to the head of Polydor Records' A&R department, Horst Schmaltze. Chandler recalled that both of them listened to the album in silence. Because of this, he was convinced Schmaltze would turn them down. But after the last track, Schmaltze confessed he had never heard anything more brilliant. He became one of the band's biggest supporters. Only seven months earlier, Jimi had been an aspiring musician eking out a living in Greenwich Village. Now he was in London, in the middle of a rock revolution and at the helm of a rising counterculture. His childhood dreams finally seemed within reach. May 5 saw the release of the band's third single, "The Wind Cries Mary," which was inspired by Jimi's girlfriend at the time, Kathy Etchingham (although there were likely many other girlfriends in Jimi's orbit). The single was released on May 12, while the band's preceding single, "Purple Haze," was still on the charts. During the first week of June, Jimi went to see another up-and-coming rock band—Pink Floyd. The band's experimental tendencies and adventurous spirit had piqued his

Hendrix wrote his songs by combining real-life experiences with visions and dreams that found their way into his head.

interest. Indeed, his tastes in music had widened enormously since his arrival in London. He listened to music in many different genres, made by famous groups and newcomers alike. His favorite genres included blues, jazz, and modern-day rock. He also greatly enjoyed The Beatles' *Sgt. Pepper*, which had been released in late May. A few days later, Hendrix was scheduled to perform at the Saville Theatre in London, which at the time was run by The Beatles' manager, Brian Epstein. Shortly before the concert Jimi was told that all four Beatles would be at the concert, so he immediately rounded up Mitchell and Redding and convinced them that they should play something a little different. When the trio went onstage, they played a magnificent version of "Sgt. Pepper" that they had spent only a few minutes rehearsing. This was an amazing and moving tribute to The Beatles, and in particular to Paul McCartney. Not only was McCartney a great fan of Hendrix, but he had also helped convince the organizers of the Monterey Pop Festival in California (scheduled for June 16–18) that they simply had to include Hendrix and the Experience as guest artists. Hendrix was about to return to his home country, where his life had been radically different. But now he had his own band and he was making music on his own terms.

58 *The cover of the 45 rpm single "Purple Haze," in the special edition released to celebrate the 51st anniversary of the song.*

59 *The cover of the 45 rpm single "The Wind Cries Mary," which the American guitarist probably wrote for Kathy Etchingham, one of his girlfriends at the time.*

60 *This is one of the best-known portraits of Hendrix. He can be seen sporting his signature military jacket. The photograph was taken by Gerard Mankowitz.*

THE NAME OF THE GROUP WAS DIFFERENT. WAS THIS A BAND OR SOMETHING MUCH MORE?

FOR THE YOUNG THE WORLD OVER, **THE SOUND OF HENDRIX'S** guitar marked the beginning of a new age

62-63 *Jimi Hendrix arriving at Heathrow Airport in London in August of 1967 with Noel Redding and Mitch Mitchell. During this trip, the Experience was held by customs officials for almost 90 minutes. A tear gas gun owned by Mitch Mitchell was confiscated.*

64 Jimi Hendrix in his dressing room with a friend before going onstage and dazzling the audience.

65 Hendrix looking at himself in the mirror of his dressing room. During this period, some of Hendrix's old recordings with Curtis Knight were rereleased.

66-67 In 1967, the Experience performed throughout Europe. Both of these photos were taken in a park in Hamburg, Germany on March 19, 1967.

Their performance in Monterey, California was the Experience's United States debut. Back at home, Hendrix still wasn't well-known, as his band's singles hadn't sold nearly as well as they had in the UK. On the evening of June 18, a few hours before the show began, a decision still hadn't been made on which band should play first: The Who or The Jimi Hendrix Experience. Hendrix and Townshend both didn't want to decide, so they flipped a coin. The Who won and got to perform first, ending their act by destroying the stage. Then it was Hendrix's turn.

In order not to be upstaged by the preceding band, the Experience gave an explosive performance of "Wild Thing," after which Jimi set his guitar on fire. The act of destroying a guitar was nothing new. Just before the release of the album *Are You Experienced*, Hendrix's trio played a series of concerts in movie theaters around the world alongside artists such as Englebert Humperdinck, the Walker Brothers, and Cat Stevens. Hendrix destroyed many guitars during this particular tour. "The smashing routine really began by accident," Hendrix stated in an interview published in *Starting at Zero*. "I was playing in Copenhagen and I got pulled off stage. Everything was going great. I threw my guitar back onto the stage and jumped back after it. When I picked it up, there was great crack down the middle. I just lost my temper and smashed the damn thing to pieces. The crowd went mad—you'd have thought I'd found the 'lost chord' or something. After that, whenever the press was about or I got that feeling, I just did the bit again. But it isn't just for the show, and I can't explain the feeling. It's just like you want to let loose and do exactly what you want if your parents weren't watching. I'm not really a violent man, but people got the impression I was because of the act. You do this destruction thing maybe three or four times and everybody thinks you do it all the time. We only do it when we feel like it. You feel really frustrated, the music gets louder and louder, and all of sudden—crash! bang!—and everything goes up in smoke. Some nights we can be really bad. If we smash something then, it's because the instrument, which is something you dearly love, simply isn't working that night. It's not responding, so you want to kill it."

Over the years, Pete Townshend had transformed gutiar destruction into art. Hendrix, drawing inspiration from the artistic works of Gustav Metzger, wanted to do something even more spectacular.

69 *A poster for the film* Monterey Pop, *a 1968 documentary directed by DA Pennebaker about the first great festival in the history of rock. The poster is an homage to Hendrix's famous guitar-burning.*

"I'M GOING WHERE I CAN BE FREE" 1967

70 and 71 Two moments from Hendrix's performance at the Monterey Pop Festival on June, 18, 1967, in Monterey, California. The festival featured some of the decade's best-known English and American bands and marked Hendrix's return to the United States.

The Monterey Festival was one of the most important concerts of the 1960s. Hendrix's flaming guitar later became a symbol of the concert.

As Humperdinck himself has stated in interviews, on the opening night of the previously mentioned tour, Jimi decided the usual methods of guitar destruction weren't going to be enough. While onstage, he covered his guitar in lighter fluid and set it on fire. It was an incredible act, but only a few people witnessed it. Jimi repeated the gesture serveral more times during later performances, each time increasing the amount of lighter fluid he used. When Jimi burned his guitar in Monterey, he had perfected the act, and this time he unleashed it before an audience of 100,000 people, which included hundreds of journalists. Many journalists were of course impressed with the band's music, but Jimi's style and showmanship blew them away. Jimi proved he could amp up the audience even when he wasn't playing, transforming himself into an electric voodoo priest capable of speaking the language of psychedelia. In only a single performance, the band succeeded in capturing the attention of the American public.

73 *This is perhaps the best-known image of Jimi Hendrix's performance at the Monterey festival. To conclude the band's set, the guitarist poured gasoline over his guitar and set it on fire.*

IN JIMI'S VIEW, SETTING A GUITAR ON FIRE WAS A SENSUAL ACT OF REBELLION

74-75 Featured here is the 1965 Fender Stratocaster guitar that Hendrix burned in London's Finsbury Park Astoria in March of 1967. In 2008, it sold at auction for 280,000 pounds ($446,000).

After the Monterey performance, Jimi became a superstar on both sides of the Atlantic. "As long as word had not got around that the English appreciated my music, in America I was an unknown," he recalled in an interview published in *Starting at Zero*. "But now we are greeted as gods in the Village clubs. I don't do anything exceptional, yet *Life* and *Time* have suddenly begun to write about me. These are the same people that used to make fun of me. Ha-ha! Now I'm not stupid

BY THE END OF 1967, THE JIMI HENDRIX EXPERIENCE APPEARED TO BE UNSTOPPABLE

Jimi anymore, I'm Mr. Hendrix. They try to analyze me and come up with a psychiatrist's report, and it's hard for them to understand what flows in my veins. We live in different worlds. My world—that's hunger, it's the slums, raging race hatred, and the only happiness is the kind that you hold in your hand, nothing more."

The band stayed in the United States for several weeks, playing shows throughout the country, including a few with The Monkees. Jimi met most of the stars of the American rock scene (except for Bob Dylan), held jam sessions day and night, and recorded new music for Ed Chalpin despite an ongoing lawsuit he had brought against him concerning a previous contract.

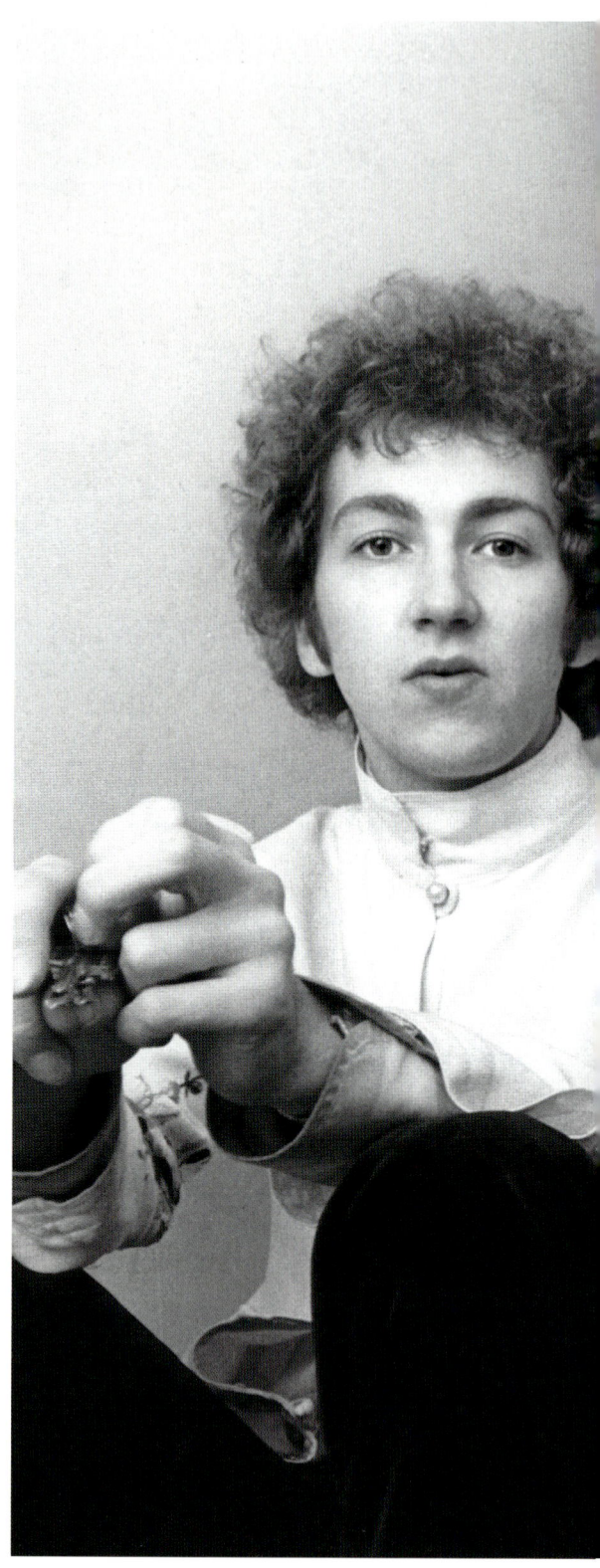

76-77 *The band backstage before their performance on one of the most popular TV shows in England: Top of the Pops, which was produced by the BBC. From left to right: Noel Redding, Mitch Mitchell, and Jimi Hendrix.*

78 July 6, 1968: The Jimi Hendrix Experience at the home of the Duke of Tavistock. From left to right: Jimi Hendrix, Noel Redding, Mitch Mitchell, DJ Emperor Rosko (Mike Pasternaki's pseudonym), and the host, Robin Russell (the Duke of Tavistock).

79 The band posing for a photograph in a forest. From left to right, Noel Redding, Jimi Hendrix, and Mitch Mitchell.

80 *Jimi Hendrix in August of 1967, when he had just become a star.*

81 *The Jimi Hendrix Experience at the peak of the band's career: Noel Redding, Jimi Hendrix, and Mitch Mitchell.*

Hendrix is known as one of the most expressive guitarists to have ever picked up the instrument

82-83 *Featured here is a classic image of Hendrix playing the guitar with his tongue, a trick he picked up early in his career, when he played in the venues making up the Chitlin' Circuit in the Deep South.*

On September 1, 1967, *Are You experienced?*, with a question mark added at the end, was released in the United States. The question mark had accidentally been omitted during the album's first printing in the UK. The album's tracklist also differed slightly from the original UK release. It contained the band's three English singles and the song "Foxey Lady," which had been changed from the original title, "Foxy Lady."

Jimi returned to England an international superstar. He wanteded to experiment further with his music, which constantly put him at odds with Chandler, who preferred that he write short, catchy singles that would play well on the radio. Hendrix was beginning to feel hampered by the three-minute limit typical of modern popular rock songs. He wanted to give free rein to his imagination and creativity, especially in the recording studio. The recording of the band's second album began almost immediately after they had finished the first album. "There was no real break," Ed Kramer recalled. "We began in May and it was like a single, continuous session. Jimi and the boys went to the studio whenever they could, between concerts, and they worked constantly." As a result, at the end of October, The Jimi Hendrix Experience's second album, *Axis: Bold as Love,* was completed. "Science-fiction rock and roll" was how Hendrix described his early work, and this description sums

84 *The cover of The Jimi Hendrix Experience's debut album,* Are You Experienced, *released in May of 1967 in the UK.*

85 *The cover of the group's second album,* Axis: Bold As Love, *released in December of 1967 in the UK.*

up the musical universe of *Axis* beautifully. Although it arrived on the heels of the first album, it demonstrated how fast Hendrix was maturing as a musician. During the recording of the first album, the trio had been working together for only a few weeks. Now that they had played some of the biggest venues in the world, their sense of musical kinship had only deepend, and each member became more attuned to the group's strengths and weaknesses. However, tension was brewing between Hendrix and Noel Redding, as Hendrix was an absolute perfectionist when it came to the bass lines of his songs. He often insisted that Noel play the songs his way, sometimes even replacing him on the bass during recordings. Another major change was Jimi's confidence. Now that he had a full studio album under his belt, he was much more familiar with the technical obstacles of translating

DESPITE THE TENSION WITH NOEL REDDING, *AXIS* IS STILL A MASTERPIECE

his experiments into recorded songs. Ed Kramer continued to be a big help in this area, along with Roger Mayer, who created many of the effects pedals Jimi used in his songs.

86 and 87 *Two photographs dating back to July 1, 1967. Jimi Hendrix plays pool in John and Michelle Phillips' Bel Air villa in Los Angeles, California.*

Jimi was still timid, but his confidence was growing. His music began to reflect this

88 Jimi Hendrix sitting on the bed of his London flat located at 23 Brook Street. He lived there for about a year with Kathy Etchingham, from 1968 to 1969.

89 Another photograph of Jimi and Kathy's London flat, which is now open to the public. The great composer George Frideric Handel lived in the building next to Hendrix's apartment during the 1700s.

HIS LYRICS
captured the dreams
of a generation in flux

90 *Jimi Hendrix writing music in his flat at 23 Brook Street, London.*

91 *A paper containing an early version of the lyrics for the song "If 6 Was 9," which Hendrix wrote in 1967.*

Even the sun is hesitant to
shine through slag filled
clouds that comes from
crowds of factories ~~spill~~ coughing
waste ~~ood~~, ~~in~~ grit and grime.
Air can be ~~made~~ clearer, but
dear me, who would dare think
of all that money to spend, ●
[bless it's little paper heart.]
Just to keep from breathing
filth and gaseous slime?

JIMI COULDN'T BREAK FREE FROM THE GHOSTS OF HIS PAST, SO HE EXORCIZED THEM THROUGH HIS MUSIC

92-93 *Jimi Hendrix performing during a television special in 1967.*

94-95 *A fine portrait of the American guitarist newly arrived in London. Former The Animals bassist Chas Chandler convinced him to come to the UK to form a band.*

95 *Hendrix in his dressing room before giving a concert at the Saville Theatre in London in June of 1967.*

The album was released on December 1, 1967, only six months after the release of the band's debut album, and the results of this relentless work ethic were truly astonishing. The album's first track, "EXP," made use of microphonic and harmonic feedback effects, creating a dizzying sound that serves as a perfect example of the "science-fiction rock and roll" Hendrix hoped to create. Throughout the album, Hendrix used stereophonic phasing techniques, shifting his guitar from one channel to another during the recording process. He turned microphonic and harmonic feedback into a kind of instrument, creating lingering buzzes and pops on many of his chords for a heavier sound. The album contains a number of Hendrix's best songs, including "If 6 Was 9," which many critics consider his masterpiece. The song is six minutes of psychedelic bliss made possible by effects such as slap echo, reverb, and fuzzbox distortion. The song "Little Wing" is one of the shorter songs on the album. Hendrix began working it while in the United States playing concerts and finished it in Monterey, California a few weeks later. The song's instrumental introduction is one of the most beautiful in rock history. The song's lyrics may refer to Native American mythology, as Hendrix was part Cherokee. In interviews, Hendrix claimed to be especially fond of "Little Wing" and the song "Angel" (the latter of which would be posthumously released on the studio album *The Cry of Love* in 1971). Both songs allude to Hendrix's mother Lucille. They're sentimental and sorrowful but also sweet and passionate. Many critics argue that *Axis: Bold As Love* is Hendrix's most autobiographical album. On the track "Spanish Castle Magic," Jimi recalls youthful visits to a nightclub in Seattle called the Spanish Castle. The song's edgy, hard-rock style made it a favorite with live audiences. The track "Castle Made of Sand" alludes to Jimi's rough childhood, his constant fear of abandonment, and the disappointments that plague everyday life. In "Up From the Skies," an alien returns to Earth for another visit, only to be dismayed by the damage and chaos created by human beings. The melancholy atmosphere of the song's lyrics won it favorable comparisons to the work of Bob Dylan. But the album isn't all dark. The playful and funky "Wait Until Tomorrow" helps lighten the mood. Although the album was received well, Hendrix's perfectionism kept him from fully appreciating it. Still, it was an enormous personal and critical success.

96-97 Jimi Hendrix photographed in profile. Here he can be seen sporting his signature bandana.

Quite famously, Hendrix lost the master tape of side one of the album, accidentally leaving it in the back seat of a London taxicab. Kramer, Chandler, and Hendrix had to remix all the songs on side one in a single night to meet the album's deadline. They were able to accomplish this feat, but Hendrix was disappointed that they couldn't get more time, as he felt that the quality of many of the tracks had suffered.

When the album was released, the band was on tour, and this tour would prove to be legendary, as it included many of the biggest bands of the day, such as The Nice with Keith Emerson, a band famous for blending rock and classical music, Roy Mood's The Move, The Amen Corner, and Pink Floyd. These bands had little to do with the beatniks and mods that had dominated Swinging London during the last decade. They were part of a new era that prized innovation, spectacular stage presence, and thoughtful lyrics. The opening show of the tour took place at the Royal Albert Hall in London and was entitled "Alchemical Wedding." The landscape of music was changing, and so was Jimi. In an interview given

English rock music was AIMING HIGHER AND BREAKING DOWN BARRIERS

to the magazine *Melody Maker* a few weeks after the release of the new album, Hendrix explained how tired he was of all the pressure thrust on his shoulders by the constant media coverage: "Do you know my biggest problem? I just can't look straight into a camera and smile if I don't feel like smiling, I just can't do it. It's like being told to be happy to order. In any case, photographers are always trying to make me look mean, and this has turned me into a sort of monster."

98 *Jimi Hendrix performing at the Royal Albert Hall in London on February 24, 1969.*

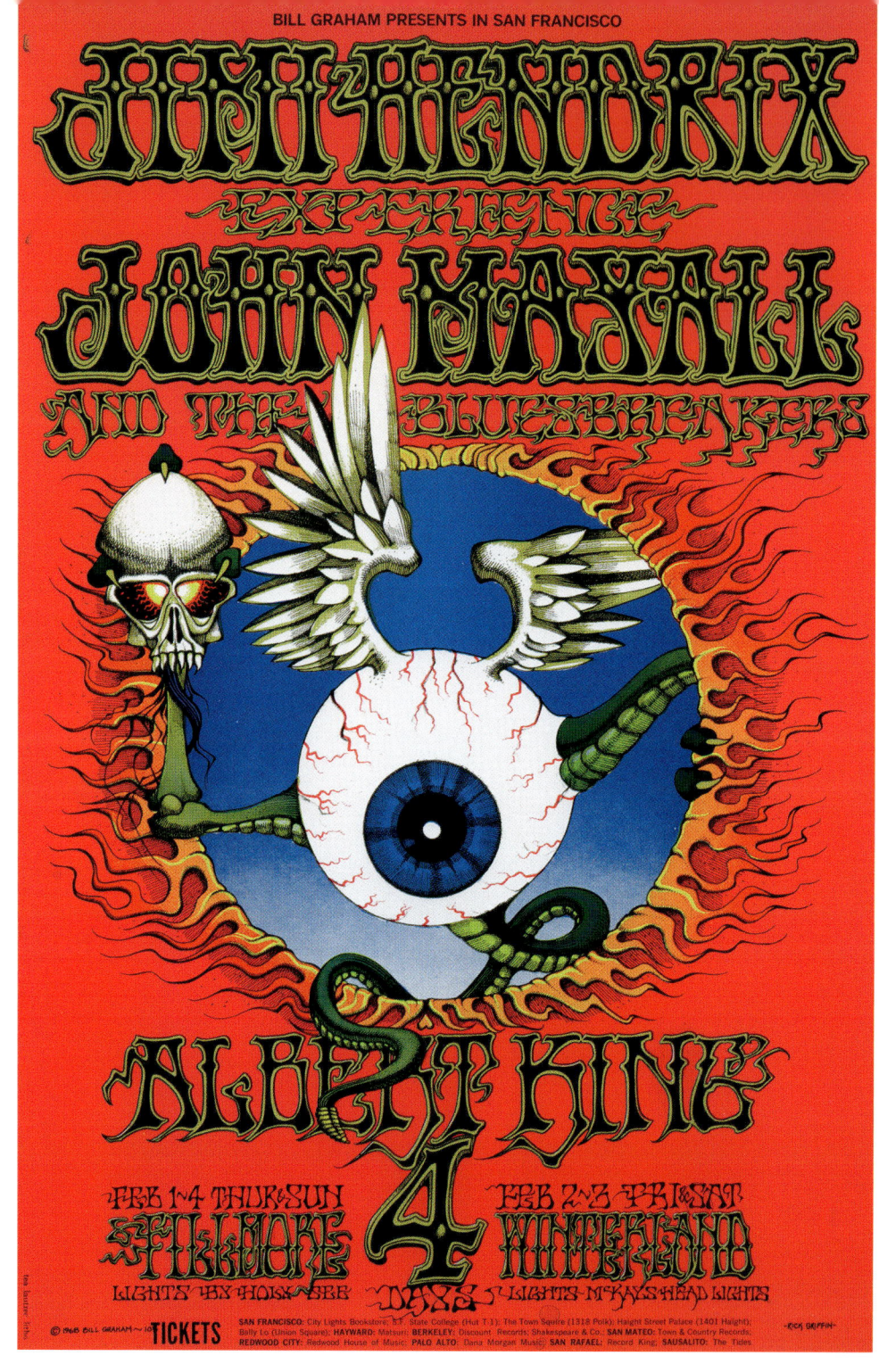

100 *A concert poster for a show featuring The Jimi Hendrix Experience, John Mayall and the Bluesbreakers, and Albert King.*

101 *A poster advertising the Joshua Light Show at the Fillmore East venue in San Francisco, California.*

He needed a break: "I'd like to take a six-month break and go to a school of music. I want to learn to read music, be a model student and study and think. I'm tired of trying to write stuff down and finding I can't." He wanted more, he wanted something better, he wanted to fly even higher, and he thought of making the band larger by keeping Mitchell and Redding and adding other musicians. In order to cope with such an uncompromising schedule, the band ramped up its drug use, favoring marijuana, amphetamines, and LSD. A plethora of drugs and women circulated backstage during their concerts. But the band was convinced they would lose their momentum if they took a break. By December of 1967, The Jimi Hendrix Experience was once again in Olympic Studios, this time recording the first tracks of their third album, *Electric Ladyland*. These songs included "Crosstown Traffic," "And the Gods Made Love," and "Little Miss Strange." In January of 1968, after a series of concerts in Sweden and Denmark, the band recorded an extraordinary version of Bob Dylan's "All Along the Watchtower." On February 1, they set off on their first headlining tour of the United States in the wake of the great success of their second album, *Axis: Bold As Love*.

Concert posters are the history books of rock and roll.

For an entire month, their concerts were sold out, and Jimi became one of the first African American stars after Otis Redding to have found fame with both white and black audiences. Despite the progress of the civil rights movement, the United States was still very much a divided nation. The year 1968 was a year of rage and protest, especially regarding the Vietnam War.

102 A 1968 portrait of Jimi Hendrix. The American guitarist achieved fame and success in the United States after his performance at the Monterey Pop Festival in Monterey, California.

1968

But this tour was also important for another reason: on February 12, Hendrix went onstage at the Center Arena in Seattle, his hometown. He hadn't been back to Seattle since 1961. A lot had changed since then. His father had remarried, and Jimi now had five more siblings. What's more, his little brother Leon had become a young man of twenty. They met at the airport, and it was a moving moment for everyone who witnessed it. They went to their father's house, and Jimi hugged Dorothy Harding and Aunt Delores. He saw Ernestine Benson again and talked music with her. And he found out that some of his dearest friends had been sent to fight in Vietnam. That evening, the whole family went to Jimi's concert, which was a big hit. The US tour continued through April. The band crossed the country and Canada, and on April 5, 1968, they reached Newark, New Jersey, where they were supposed to perform two concerts, one in the afternoon and one in the evening. But the evening concert was cancelled, as the organizers were afraid riots would break out. Dr. Martin Luther King had been assassinated in Memphis, Tennessee. The band went onstage during the afternoon concert and played in front of a sparse crowd, as many people had decided to stay home. Toward the end of the set, Jimi played a melancholy blues tune "dedicated to a friend of mine." That evening he returned to New York and went to play with Buddy Guy at the Generation Club, and once more it was blues and suffering.

1968 was a year of revolution. Young people all over the world took to the streets to protest against a society they no longer wanted.

Jimi had never paid much attention to civil rights or politics, but between 1967 and 1968, his social consciousness expanded enormously. He began to wear anti-war pins, and in interviews he spoke constantly of peace and racial integration. His music became more socially committed and "serious" while he was preparing the songs for the band's third album, *Electric Ladyland*. But politics as such didn't really interest him. He felt close to the battles waged by the youth movement and the civil rights movement, but the frontlines of the Yippies and the Black Panthers weren't where he felt most comfortable, as he explained in an interview published in the book *Starting at Zero*: "They asked us to give benefit concerts for the Black Panthers, which I was really very happy to do for them. I was honored and all that, but. . . in the USA, you have to decide which side you're on. You are either a rebel or you're a Frank Sinatra type. When I was younger, I would write protest songs full of rancor. I don't do that now because there are political matters I just prefer to ignore. Before stating anything, I must feel involved. I don't feel involved. I feel almost completely lost now, sometimes from almost everything. I feel sorry for the minorities, but I don't feel part of one. I'm for the masses. Race isn't a problem in my world. I don't look at things in terms of races. I look at things in terms of people. I'm not thinking about black people or white people. I'm thinking about the obsolete and the new. It isn't that I'm not relating to the Black Panthers. I naturally feel a part of what they're doing, in certain respects. Somebody has to make a move, and we're the ones hurting most as far as peace of mind and living are concerned. . . .But I'm not for guerilla warfare. Not frustrated things like throwing little cocktail bottles here and there or breaking up a store window.

That's nothing. Especially in your own neighborhood. I don't feel hate for anybody, because that's nothing but taking two steps back.... Other people have no legs or no eyesight or have fought in wars. You should feel sorry for them and think what part of their personality they have lost. It's good when you start adding up universal thoughts."

Work on *Electric Ladyland* continued at Record Plant Studios in New York through April and May of 1968, but the mood and atmosphere were much different than during the band's previous recording sessions. Hendrix wanted to achieve a level of musical perfection that had eluded him during the makings of his two previous albums. This time he would do everything his own way, without the advice of Chandler, Mitchell, or Redding. But his chaotic lifestyle made for a difficult working environment. He was always hovering between the studio and New York's many clubs and bars, especially the Generation Club in Greenwich Village, which was rife with drugs and young people. Jimi would leave the clubs followed by swarms of people, and inevitably he would invite some of them back to the studio, which complicated the lives of his bandmates and the studio's sound engineers. Ofentimes, Hendrix would spend hours perfecting a particular track, only to scrap it entirely in favor of something improvised. Chandler became fed up with this state of affairs and decided to leave his position as producer. An account from Jefferson Airplane bassist Jack Casady offers a clearer picture into Hendrix's working methods: "I recall the recording of 'Voodoo Chile.' We were at the Scene club, where there was a jam session with Jimi. When the club closed, he invited us all to go with him to Record Plant Studios, there must have been about twenty persons, only a few were musicians, while the others were at the club for fun and came with us. At 7:30 in the morning, we began to record, with me at the bass, Jimi playing guitar, Steve Winwood at the keyboards, and Mitch Mitchell played drums. It was all very spontaneous, and we made three recordings, then I had to go, I had another concert that same evening and had to rest for a few hours." The song, which is 15 minutes long, became one of Hendrix's classics. His power, spontaneity, and incredible intensity all seemed present in these magical moments. But Chas Chandler, the person who had opened the door to success for Jimi, the musician who had understood his genius and who had taken him to England to start a new life, was no longer his producer or manager. Michael Jeffrey decided to buy Chandler out, and the latter had no further professional contact with Hendrix.

To a certain extent this, was a problem. Not because of Jimi's studio skills (he was known to be a whiz behind the soundboard, and he still had Ed Kramer to support him), but because without Chandler, Jimi no longer had anyone in his orbit to question or challenge his creative decisions. Hendrix was now surrounded by yes-men and by people who tended to idolize him . And of course his drug use was becoming a bigger issue, especially in the case of LSD, which played an important role in helping him escape from the pressures brought on by his daily life. He also believed it helped him creatively, but he was constantly upping his dosage in pursuit of the drug's full effects. By the middle of 1968, Jimi no longer had a real home. He spent less and less time in London, in the apartment he had lived in with Kathy Etchingham on Brook Street, in the heart of the city. Jimi was now working mostly in the United States, playing in larger venues and earning much more money than he had in the UK. Jeffrey went as far as to close the London office where he had originally organized the guitarist's activities. Economically, things were going splendidly for the band. The earnings from their concerts and album sales were considerable, but so were their expenses, a great many of which were probably unnecessary. Because of his high earnings, Jimi wanted to take his time with this third album, halting work on it entirely during times when the band was on tour.

He also had a passion project in mind: the creation of a perfect recording studio just for him—a place without budget restrictions or technical limitations and that wasn't controlled by a record company. The studio would always be at his disposal, meaning he wouldn't have to worry about squeezing studio time in between concerts and tours. He began scouting out locations in New York for his dream studio, hoping to call it Electric Lady Studios. The project was eventually completed in 1970, but it would take double the amount of time and money originally expected. Hendrix was unable to record *Electric Ladyland* in Electric Lady Studios, as it wasn't ready in time, but after an initial recording session back in England and another in Sound Center Studios in New York, he settled on using Record Plant Studios to record his third album. Immediatley he set to work rerecording songs the band had recorded back in England.

Another reason Jimi wanted his own studio was because of his working habits, which made recording sessions in normal studios expensive. Hendrix often insisted on dozens of takes per song, always aiming for perfection.

"HAVE YOU EVER BEEN TO ELECTRIC LADYLAND? THE MAGIC CARPET WAITS FOR YOU, SO DON'T BE LATE"

104 *Jimi Hendrix holding the cover of* Electric Ladyland *while sitting in his London flat in January of 1969.*

Electric Ladyland

the Jimi Hendrix Experience

STEREO

6307

...AND THE GODS MADE LOVE
HAVE YOU EVER BEEN (TO ELECTRIC LADYLAND)
CROSSTOWN TRAFFIC
VOODOO CHILE

LITTLE MISS STRANGE
LONG HOT SUMMER NIGHT
COME ON (PART 1)
GYPSY EYES
BURNING OF THE MIDNIGHT LAMP

RAINY DAY, DREAM AWAY
1983... (A MERMAN I SHOULD TURN TO BE)
MOON, TURN THE TIDES... gently gently away

STILL RAINING, STILL DREAMING
HOUSE BURNING DOWN
ALL ALONG THE WATCHTOWER
VOODOO CHILD (SLIGHT RETURN)

106 and 107 Three different covers of the double album Electric Ladyland, released worldwide in the fall of 1968. Because of the cover's nudity, many record shops refused to stock the album.

HENDRIX WASN'T A POLITICAL ACTIVIST, BUT HE SUPPORTED THE CIVIL RIGHTS MOVEMENT AND SPOKE OUT AGAINST THE VIETNAM WAR

108 *Jimi Hendrix during a concert on February 24, 1969, at the Royal Albert Hall in London. The band ended its most recent European tour with two concerts on February 18 and February 24, the only occasions in which Hendrix played this famous venue.*

110 Another moment from Jimi Hendrix's February 24, 1969 concert at the Royal Albert Hall in London. Hendrix is laser-focused on his guitar.

Many different musicians were featured on ELECTRIC LADYLAND. Jimi's band was getting bigger

113 *Jimi Hendrix pretending to hitchhike while at Heathrow Airport in London. The guitarist was about to take a private plane to the Isle of Wight, where he was set to perform at the famous Isle of Wight Festival.*

According to Hendrix lore, the band went through 43 different takes to record the song "Gypsy Eyes." And in order to get just the right acoustic guitar sound on "All Along the Watchtower," Hendrix insisted that Dave Mason (of the band Traffic) record 20 different takes. *Electric Ladyland* is attributed to The Experience as a complete band, but in many ways it was really Jimi's album from start to finish, including from a production standpoint. Tension between the band's members reached its peak shortly before they began recording the album. Noel Redding and Hendrix argued frequently, unable to agree on anything. A parcitularly nasty argument almost came to blows while the band was touring Scandinavia. Later that night, Jimi destroyed his Stockholm hotel room in a drug-and-booze-fueled rage and ended up in jail for a night (an incident referred to in the song "My Friend," which was released posthumously). Redding, who during this period had formed his own

In the recording studio with Ed Kramer, HENDRIX MADE his dreams come true

band, Fat Mattress, couldn't stand Hendrix's relentless pace, mood swings, and changing artistic visions, and he frequently left the recording studio in order to calm down. But ofentimes, when he returned, he found that his bass parts had been rerecorded by Hendrix himself. Examples of this include the recordings of "All Along the Watchtower" and "1983... (A Merman I Should Turn to Be)." In many other cases, such as the song "Voodoo Chile," Redding didn't even bother putting down a bass line. But Redding did write and sing the lead on one of the album's most successful tracks: "Little Miss Strange." *Electric Ladyland* was thus only partly recorded by The Experience's other two members. Many other musicians took part in the sessions, including Steve Winwood, Dave Mason, and Chris Wood of the band Traffic, Al Kooper, Jimi's old friend Buddy Miles, and even Brian Jones, who played the drums on an alternate version of "Voodoo Chile" that was released posthumously.

114 *Hendrix working behind the mixing board in the sound room of Electric Lady Studios in New York on June 17, 1970. Jimi sits next to the American sound engineer Eddie Kramer (born in South Africa). To his right is the studio's manager, Jim Marron.*

4
THE WOMEN IN JIMI'S LIFE

**FROM SEATTLE TO LONDON TO NEW YORK,
JIMI WAS ALWAYS
LOOKING FOR LOVE**

It was no accident that Jimi's new album was titled *Electric Ladyland*. For better or worse, women were always at the center of Hendrix's world. Hendrix liked women quite a lot. He was polite, sweet, and passionate, which obviously worked in his favor when courting someone new. He never had any difficulties in finding a girlfriend, but at the same time, it can't be said he ever committed himself fully to one woman. Without a doubt, the most important woman in his life had been his mother, Lucille. Love and abandonment went hand in hand in Hendrix's mind due to his personal experiences with his mother, which of course were painful and complicated. The angel Hendrix sang about in the song "Little Wing" is an idealized female figure who follows and protects him while observing him from the heavens. Hendrix's relationships tended to be intense, constantly

LOVE AND ABANDONMENT WENT HAND IN HAND for Jimi Hendrix.

changing, volatile, uncertain, unstable, and full of passion. He surrounded himself with women and wrote many songs alluding to female figures, but none of them ever truly possessed him, and by the end of his life, he had left a long trail of broken hearts.

Yet women were a fundamental part of his success, beginning with Linda Keith, who played a major role in his decision to move to England. There was Kathy Etchingham, of course, whom Hendrix shared an apartment with in London for almost a year. Despite Jimi's dalliances with other women, the two remained in a relationship of sorts for several years. Indeed, Jimi occasionally told the press that Kathy was his fiancée. But obviously this wasn't true. Kathy certainly played an important role in his life, but by 1969, she could no longer bear Jimi's unending stream of "electric ladies."

Gangs of groupies always seemed to flock to Jimi, whether he was backstage at a concert or sitting alone on a park bench. There were women with him in his hotel rooms, on his tour buses, and even in the recording studio. In many cases, they crowded out his real friends, which created a host of personal problems. Often, it felt like Jimi chased women to fill a void in his life. Quite famously, he had a relationship with Devon Wilson. The two reportedly bonded over their troubled childhoods. They first met in 1965 and had an open, on-again-off-again relationship. But because Wilson was one of the few constants in Jimi's life, many of his friends saw her as a life companion of sorts.

Wilson was know to have had relationships with many other rockstars, including Brian Jones, Mick Jagger, Eric Clapton, Duane Allman, Miles Davis, and Quincy Jones. She was accepting of Jimi's relationships with other women and eventually became his personal assistant, accompanying him to the studio on many occasions.

120 and 121 *Two portraits of the lovely English model Linda Keith, who for a while was the girlfriend of Keith Richards of the Rolling Stones. She also had brief relationship with Hendrix. She is credited with introducing Jimi to Chas Chandler of the band The Animals.*

KATHY ETCHINGHAM WAS THE ONLY WOMAN HENDRIX EVER CONSIDERED MARRYING

122-123 and 123 *Jimi Hendrix and Kathy Etchingham in their Brook Street flat in the Mayfair district of London. The guitarist's relationship with Etchingham may have been his most consistent romantic relationship.*

But Hendrix's relationship with Devon wasn't simple. She could at times be controlling, positioning herself as Jimi's gatekeeper and keeping people she didn't like away from him. She wanted to play an important role in his life, sometimes growing jealous of the other women he saw, including Kathy Etchingham. Any problems the two had were of course complicated by drugs, alcohol, and constant partying. A steady supply of hard drugs seemed to be affecting Hendrix's personality. He lost many friendships in the months leading up to his death. And many of his fellow musicians could hardly stand Wilson's presence, especially in the recording studio, where she frequently interferred with the work at hand. It was also widely believed that Wilson was vindictive. In order to punish people she didn't like, she supposedly spiked their drinks with LSD when they weren't paying attention. Two of Hendrix's songs are thought to allude to Devon Wilson: "Dolly Dagger," and "Freedom." Jimi's relationships with Kathy Etchingham and Devon Wilson perfectly illustrate the way his outlook about romance seemed to change between his time in London and his masive success in the United States. The more money, acclaim, and freedom Hendrix gained, the more unstable and toxic his relationships seemed to become. It was almost as though Electric Ladyland were inhabited by ghost ladies instead of real ones.

His relationships with women became increasingly unstable and impersonal. Jimi seemed to want ghosts instead of romantic partners.

125 *Jimi Hendrix with Devon Wilson at the Winter Concert for Peace, which took place at Madison Square Garden on January 28, 1970.*

Another important woman in Jimi's life was Monika Dannemann. She was the last person to see Hendrix alive. The two met at a concert in Düsseldorf in January of 1969 and saw each other several times throughout the year. Although she played only a small role in Hendrix's life, she was present with him during his last night on Earth.

Despite his emotional instability, Hendrix WAS A PASSIONATE LOVER always looking for a new connection

In most instances, Hendrix formed relationships with women purely on the magic of the moment. If he met a woman who he wanted to be with (and who wanted to be with him), he acted without hesitation, living life to the fullest. It may be fair to say he fell in love with all of them, as many claimed that he had talked to them about marriage. These "engagements" may have lasted only a few hours (or less), but that didn't lessen their passion or intensity.

127 *The German figure skater and painter Monika Dannemann, who was Jimi Hendrix's last girlfriend. He was with her at the Samarkand Hotel in the Notting Hill Gate area of London the night he died.*

5 THE GUITAR

JIMI'S SPACESHIP HAD SIX STRINGS AND A WHAMMY BAR

By January of 1969, Hendrix was tired of London, those three-minute tracks everyone wanted him to record, and his interactions with record company executives. He'd had enough of the continuous touring and the other members of The Experience. In April of 1968, Hendrix abandoned everything and left for New York to finish recording *Electric Ladyland*. He brought the master tracks the band had recorded during their sessions in London. Chas Chandler was still in the picture as Jimi's manager. Up until now, he had been able to keep Hendrix within the 3-4 minute song format, which many in the music business considered the ideal format for a successful rock song, but this was changing, and Chandler's days as Jimi's manager were numbered. During the recording sessions at Record Plant Studios in New York, Hendrix exerted more and more control over all operations, listening more to his own creative instincts than to his managers, his bandmates, or the studio's sound engineers. He continued to evolve as a guitarist, keeping up his search for new sounds and new ways of incorporating distortion and noise into his songs. The masterpieces "Crosstown Traffic" and "All Along the Watchtower" were mostly recorded in London, while "1983... (A Merman I Should Turn to Be)" and the fifteen-minute psychedelic explosion "Voodoo Chile" were recorded in New York. However, the album's songs still feel interconnected despite the chaos of the recording process. They're an impressive snapshot of Hendrix's evolution as an artist. He could have settled into his role

HENDRIX USED HIS GUITAR LIKE A KALEIDOSCOPE, HOPING TO SEE THE WORLD DIFFERENTLY

as lead guitarist and vocalist and left the songwriting and studio techniques to other people, but in his quest for total creative freedom, he decided to master those other key aspects of songmaking as well. *Electric Ladyland* is strong evidence that he succeeded.

Hendrix was clearly searching for a more profound means of expression, a sentiment he repeated many times during media interviews. He stated that he didn't want to merely play music, he wanted to try to glimpse his real character through his music, to express himself on a deeper level and attain something truly spiritual. It's difficult to imagine a more sensual or desperately physical guitarist than Jimi Hendrix. Passion, beauty, and vision are merged together in his playing in an attempt to establish spiritual contact with the audience. The album *Electric Ladyland* has been described by critics as "electric gospel," "Technicolor music," "cyber blues," and "psychedelic pop," but whatever its genre, it's a fantastic, visionary album full of hard-to-define tracks that combine social commentary and catchy rhythms. The word "psychedelic" comes from the ancient Greek words *psyche* (soul) and *delos* (clear). Thus the album can be seen as the most complete and transparent manifestation of the soul of James Marshall Hendrix, a rock guitarist from Seattle and the first and greatest guitar hero in the strange genre of psychedelic rock.

1968 was of course a tumultuous year. In the United States, counterculture and youth movements were changing everything, and the rest of the country (and the world) were trying to catch up. Hendrix's music merged beautifully with the chaos of the times, reaching out warmly towards the new and shunning everything that reaked of stale tradition.

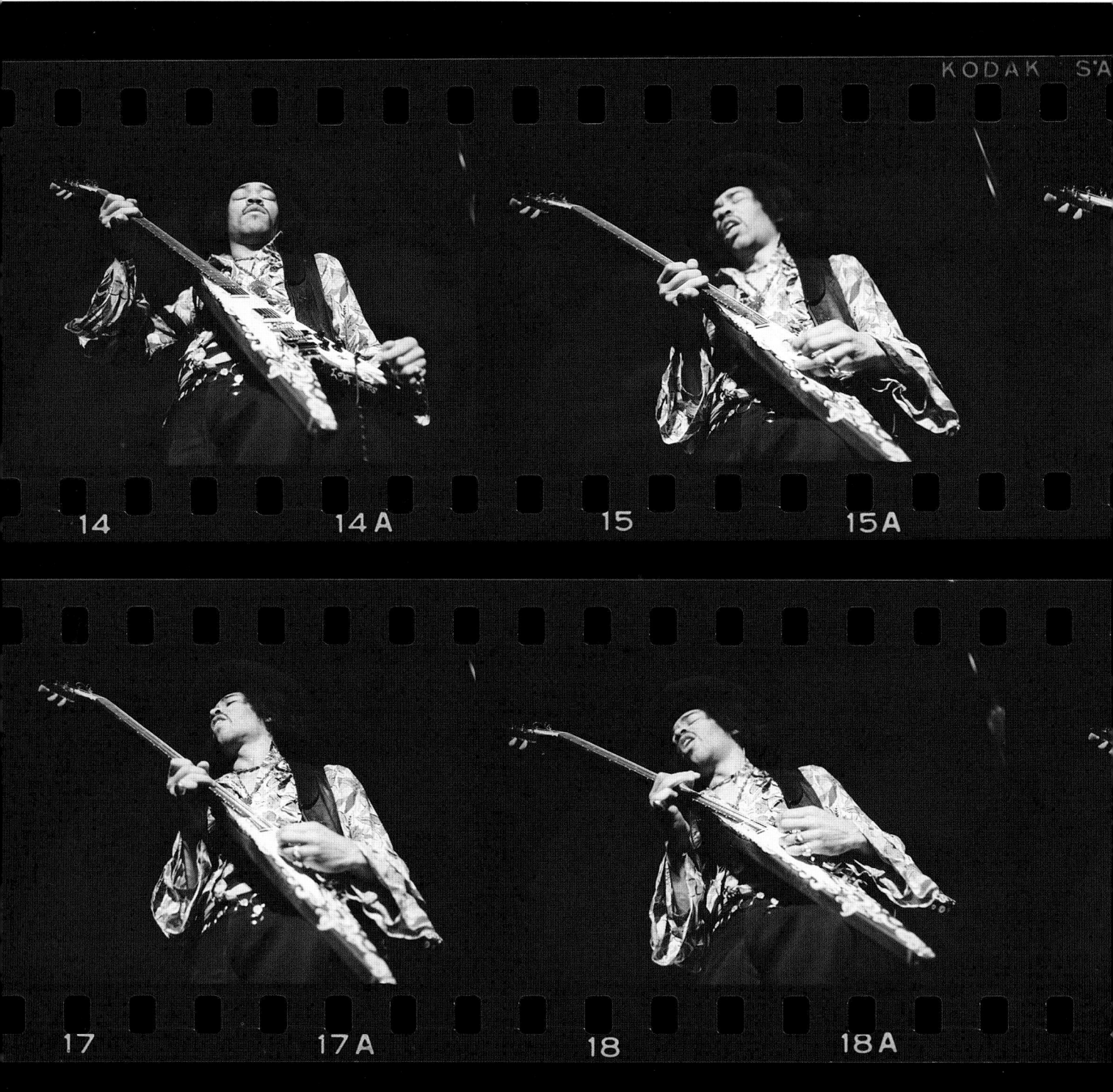

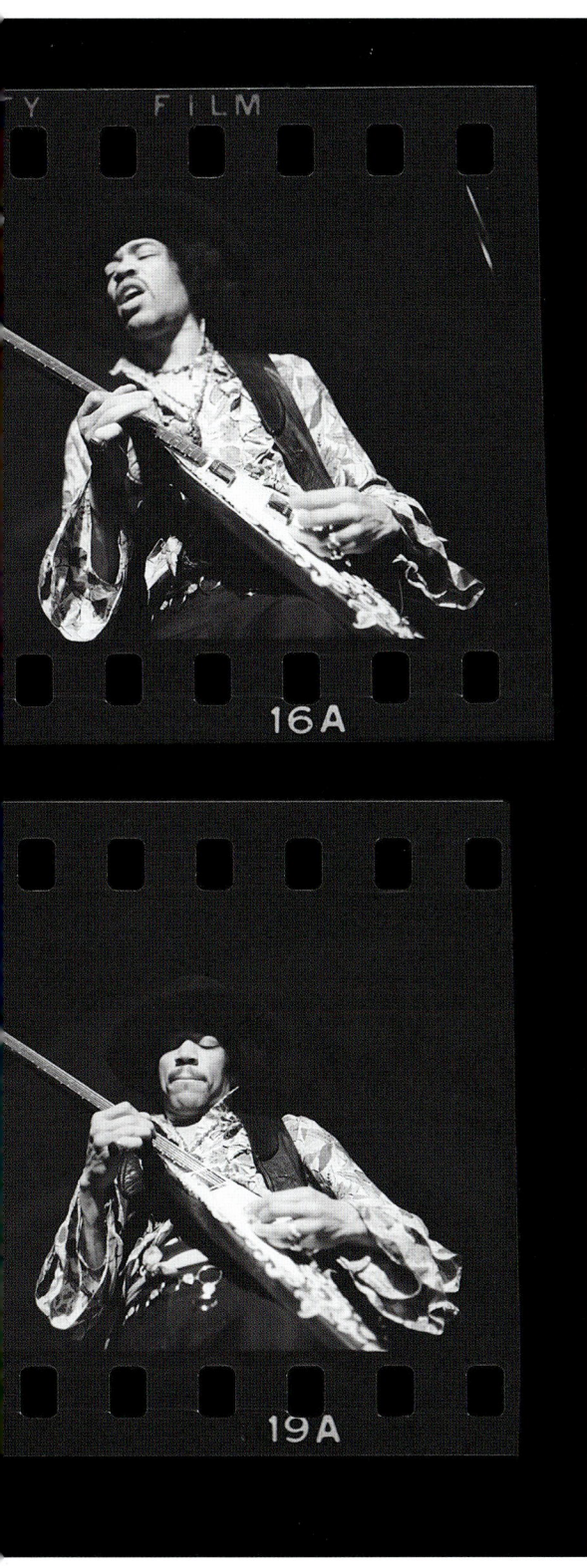

THROUGH HIS GUITAR PLAYING, HENDRIX HOPED TO IMITATE THE SOUNDS OF GODS MAKING LOVE

In his book *Freakshow*, music academic Albert Goldman relates his meeting with Hendrix at the Drake Hotel in New York, during which the guitarist allowed him listen to the still-unfinished tapes of *Electric Ladyland* for the first time. It's an interesting glimpse into how Hendrix himself viewed his incomplete music. Hendrix talked about his use of noise and his attempts to interweave notes and sounds to mimic "the gods when they make love." In Hendrix's view, rock music was first all about the body. Later it became obsessed with the mind. Hendrix wanted to use his music to combine the two. *Electric Ladyland* certainly feels that way, with its catchy tunes and deep lyrics. It lands somewhere between the electricity of the future and the primal sounds of the first humans. As Goldman writes, the act of listening to the album was like "walking around in an art gallery admiring a series of masterpieces."

132-133 *Prints taken by the photographer Baron Wolman during Hendrix's concert at the Winterland Ballroom in San Francisco on February 4, 1968.*

These masterpieces extended the frontiers of rock beyond what other great musicians had achieved up until 1968. Hendrix used the recording studio the same way a sculptor uses a hammer and chisel. Every new sound was studied and obsessed over, and every detail of every song had to be just right. "The idea of Hendrix as the 'wild man' of pop is totally wrong," stated Eddie Kramer, Hendrix's most dedicated sound engineer and his collaborator on the albums *Are You Experienced* and *Axis: Bold As Love*. "Jimi was absolutely in control of all the material and prepared everything with precision and a great deal of calculation, up to the last note of a solo in reverse. He was marvelous at the console and chose the musicians who would work with him with the same careful thought. There was nothing casual in his work."

Hendrix was a mad scientist. EVERY SONG WAS an attempt at something new

Reality in Hendrix's *Electric Ladyland* is multidimensional, and there are many ways to interpret each song. Many utilize simple licks and chord progressions, but their lyrics and effects add layers of meaning. This pecliar tension is what makes this album so exhilarating to listen to.

Hendrix never offered pure comfort or certainty. Instead, he gave listeners the ability to choose their own meanings and the permission to transform themselves. Without a doubt, *Electric Ladyland* represents the peak

THE INVENTIVENESS OF HENDRIX'S GUITAR CONTINUES TO INSPIRE BUDDING GUITARISTS

of his career as a musician. At last he had attained total independent creativity. Each song on the album was an experiment in itself, so it's hard to say exactly where Hendrix would have taken his music had he lived longer. Would he have continued further into psychedelia, or would he have pared his tracks down and focused more on his solos? Whatever the possibilities, one thing is certain: his guitar would have been at the forefront of his musical development. He was constantly discovering new depths to reach with this incredibly rich instrument, and it's interesting to think about where he would have taken his legendary guitar skills if he had made another album.

Electric Ladyland was released in September of 1968. Within a few weeks, it shot to number one on the US charts. Hendrix had conquered rock music. The foundation of the album was the inventiveness of his guitar playing. He presided over each track like a conductor over an orchestra. Hendrix's use of distortion, echoes, delay, flangers, and a thousand other gadgets and devices modified the sound of his instrument in ways that didn't feel gimmicky or shallow. He seemed to have an entire universe in his hands instead of six strings. Indeed, his intricate solo work always seemed to push the limits of what could be achieved on a guitar with a single pair of hands. But perfect technique was never an end in itself. If something in one of his songs sounded too clean or manufactured, Jimi would give it an edge with a new effect or a new swirl of notes. He is thus remembered as one of the guitar's most inventive practitioners. And of course all of this is even more astounding given his humble beginnings. Hendrix seemed to embody the spirit of modernist painters like Pablo Picasso or Marc Chagall in that he combined traditional techniques with a bold new vision. In 1967, he put aside his usual approach to the guitar and began playing as though he were a curious extraterrestrial.

137 *A photograph from Jimi Hendrix's last concert, which was held on September 6, 1970 on the island of Fehmarn in Germany. Hendrix died only a few days later.*

"Nowadays it is perhaps more difficult to understand, because everything has been assimilated, digested, transformed into the obvious," writes Italian music journalist Gino Castaldo. "But at that time, when people first grasped the subversive power of that guitar, everything that Hendrix did had the provocative flavor of the new, and it was precisely this that represented the rebellious and implacable spirit of the time. From that first obscure, mysterious blue cadence in 'Hey Joe' to the astounding 'sea changes' of 'If 6 Was 9,' and from the tenderness veined with psychedelia in 'Little Wing' to the highly personal, subjective quality of *Electric Ladyland*, his music always had the fascination of a new frontier that was continuously revamped, piece after piece. Hendrix seemed to be chasing after something more and more imaginative, unrealizable, and utopian, in a deafening kaleidoscope basically performed with only one voice and one guitar."

Hendrix has no real imitators. No one after him was able to transform the guitar in such a radical manner.

It's no accident that Hendrix has no real imitators or successors. It's hard to identify any "Hendrixian" guitarists after him. Other guitarists, even the best of the best, continue to play the guitar well, but they seem to lack the emotional connection Hendrix had to his instrument. They also can't seem to blend genres and styles as smoothly as he could.

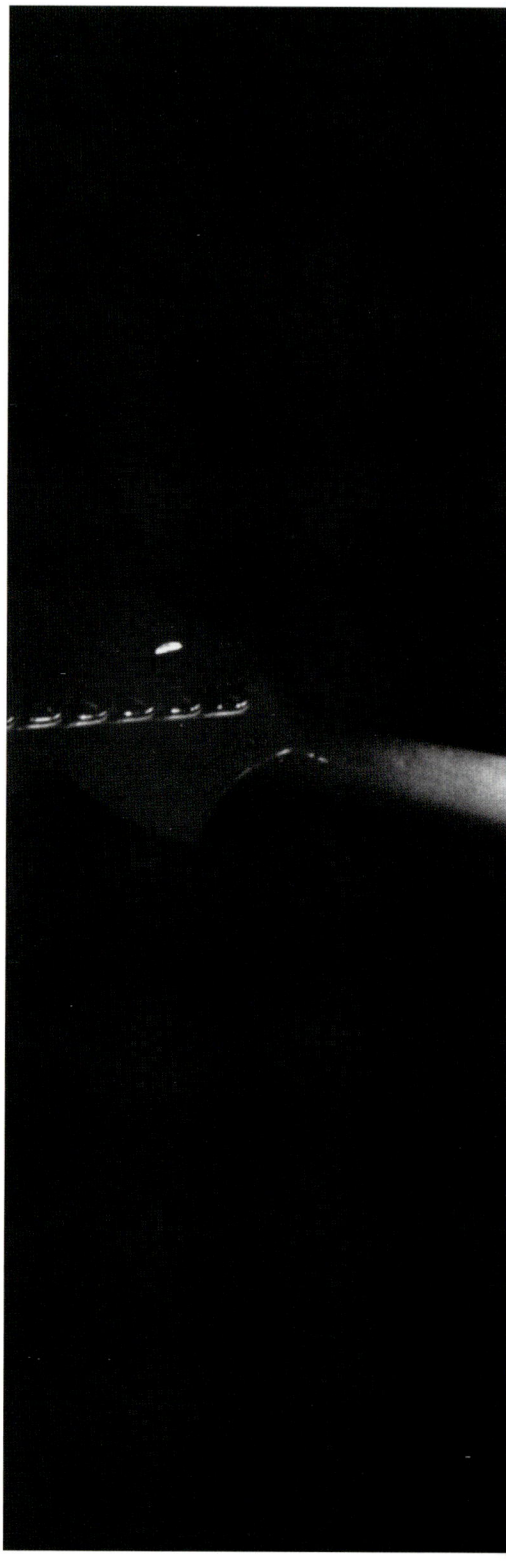

138-139 *Hendrix playing the guitar with his tongue during the historic Monterey Pop Festival in Monterey, California. The festival was held on June 18, 1967. It marked the beginning of Hendrix's fame in the United States.*

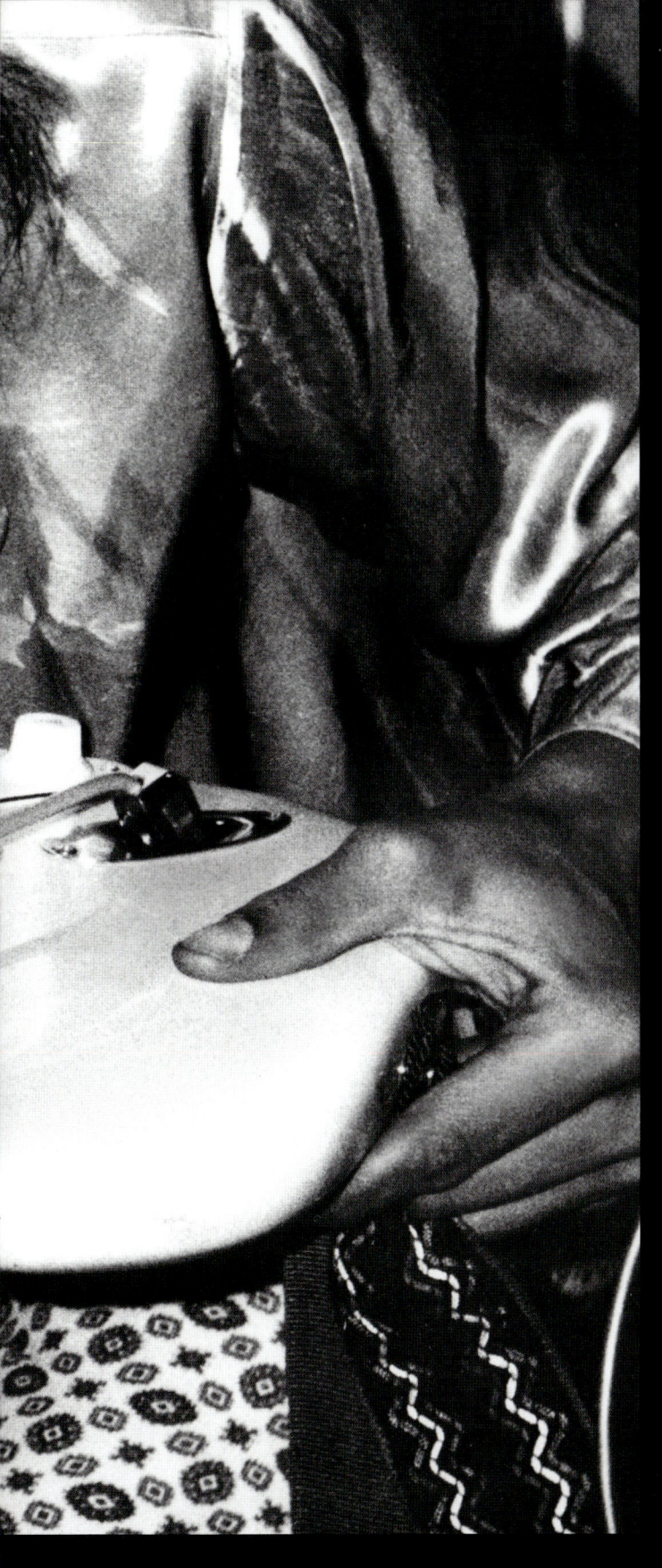

140-141 Jimi Hendrix performing at the Monterey Pop Festival on June 18, 1967.

142-143 Hendrix showing off one of his many guitar tricks during a performance in Munich, Germany.

144-145 *Jimi Hendrix about to destroy one of his guitars. He and Pete Townshend of the band The Who were famous for smashing their guitars onstage at the end of shows, which drove audiences wild.*

JIMI COULD PLAY WITH HIS TEETH, HIS TONGUE, BEHIND HIS BACK, AND BETWEEN HIS LEGS

146 and 147 *Two photographs of Jimi Hendrix playing during one of his last concerts, held on June 27, 1970 at Boston Garden in Boston, Massachusetts.*

148 and 149 Two more photographs of Jimi Hendrix performing at the Isle of Wight Festival, which took place August 26–30, 1970. The festival also featured The Doors, The Who, Joni Mitchell, Miles Davis, Jethro Tull, Free, Ten Years After, Joan Baez, The Moody Blues, Donovan, Emerson, Lake & Palmer, Leonard Cohen, Taste, and many others.

EVERY GUITAR SOLO REVEALED A PIECE OF JIMI'S SOUL

150 and 151 *Three moments from Hendrix's concert at the K.B. Hallen arena in Copenhagen, Denmark on September 3, 1970. This was one of the great American guitarist's last shows. At the end of his last European tour, Hendrix returned to London, where he died on September 18.*

HENDRIX USED THE SIX STRINGS OF HIS GUITAR TO CHANGE MUSIC FOREVER

152 Featured here are photo prints from one of Hendrix's many concerts. While performing live, he and his bandmates loved to improvise. In fact, their live renditions of the songs in their own repertoire often differed wildly from the recordings.

153 Jimi Hendrix onstage at the Isle of Wight Festival in England (August 1970). This was one of the great guitarist's last live performances.

JIMI HELPED TRANSFORM THE GUITAR INTO A SYMBOL OF YOUTH CULTURE

154 A studio photograph of Jimi's 1967 Gibson Flying V guitar. It was one of many guitars he used during his live performances.

155 Hendrix onstage with his Flying V at the Fifth Dimension Club in Ann Arbor, Michigan, on August 15, 1967.

156 and 157 Three of the guitars Hendrix played during his short career. Hendrix flipped the white guitar over and reversed the strings.

158-159 Close-up of Hendrix's hands during a concert at the Falkoner Center in Copenhagen, Denmark on January 10, 1969.

6 THE END

ICARUS FLEW TOO CLOSE TO THE SUN, BUT AT LEAST HE FLEW

The band returned to London at the end of their 1968 American tour. Throughout this period, Jimi and Noel's arguments had become increasingly heated. Jimi had been absent from London for six months. He reunited with Kathy Etchingham at the Brook Street apartment. In various media appearances, he referred to her as his "Yoko Ono." By the time The Experience was ready for another tour, the situation was completely different. The band was no longer united. The positive atmosphere had been replaced by a slow-burning tension, and drug consumption had become constant for all three members. Hendrix was surrounded by drugs of all kinds. It may not be fair to say he was addicted to any specific drug, but there were few

The more Hendrix relied on drugs AND ALCOHOL, THE MORE ALONE HE BECAME

days now when he didn't have some kind of drug in his system. But drugs weren't actually Hendrix's main problem. Alcohol was always the greater danger for him, because when Jimi drank, he often lost control of himself and became another person. And of course both of his parents had struggled with alcohol dependency. Eric Burdon, the front man of the band The Animals, recalled how shocking it was to see Jimi drunk. The amiable, polite, passionate person he knew would transform into a violent and cold man. When he drank, he would destroy hotel rooms, bars, clubs, or the living rooms of friends. Naturally many of Hendrix's friendships suffered because of his drinking habits.

When the band's European tour ended, Hendrix spent three weeks in London. In mid-March, returned to the United States, where he was joined by Kathy Etchingham the following week. But this arrangement didn't last long, as Kathy couldn't stand the direction Jimi's life was taking. His entourage of friends now seemed to include only hangers-on and large numbers of groupies willing to put up with whatever Hendrix said or did. In Charles Cross's book *Room Full of Mirrors*, Kathy Etchingham describes encountering a man in Jimi's apartment sporting a raincoat and roaming around the apartment with a large bag of cocaine and a loaded pistol. This was the last straw for her. She left Hendrix for good and went back to London.

The band's new American tour began in April of 1969. It would be 20 shows and include a total of 350,000 spectators. The proceeds would amount to roughly $1,300,000. Racial tensions in the United States had reached their peak, and large concerts could quickly turn into violent brawls. The FBI had even decided to start a file on Hendrix, investigating his relationship with the Black Power Movement.

164 Jimi Hendrix's mug shot from his arrest in Toronto, Canada. He was arrested at the Canadian border on May 3, 1969 for drug possession.

1969

Things only got worse in May, when Hendrix was arrested at the Canadian border for marijuana and heroin possession. Jimi denied the drugs were his, but he was charged with possessing them all the same. The trial was set for the month of December. The band resumed its tour, but a couple of weeks later, during an interview in Los Angeles, Hendrix declared that his next tour wouldn't include his Experience bandmates. He hadn't talked to anyone about this idea. Noel and Mitch were left totally in the dark about his future plans. The band played a few more concerts, the last being in Denver, Colorado. The famous trio made up of Noel Redding, Mitch Mitchell, and Jimi Hendrix would never perform together again.

Hendrix continued making music. He wanted to move forward with his career. He called up his old buddy Billy Cox and, together with Mitch Mitchell, started a new band. Hendrix considered this group the core of what would eventually become a much larger band with more instruments, which would expand the range of sounds they could produce during shows. By this time, Hendrix had also become interested in subjects such as art, philosophy, and history. He was seeking new horizons and new limits to transcend, especially within himself. He made a brief trip to Morocco, where he learned about African culture. He asked another guitarist to join the band—Larry Lee, with whom he had played years, before during his Nashville days. He also added two new percussionists: Jerry Venezia and Juma Sultan. This was a new era for Hendrix, and he planned to give priority to acoustic instruments during live shows. He lived for a short while in Woodstock, New York, a town roughly 108 miles outside of New York City. Many other musicians—the first and foremost being Bob Dylan—had also put down roots there.

"I want to show them that music is universal—that there is no white rock or black rock."

Because of this, it was only natural that he should accept an invitation extended to him by concert promoter Michael Lang, whom Hendrix had met the year before, at the Miami Pop Festival in Miami, Florida, to participate in the Woodstock Music and Art Fair set for August 15-18, 1969. Hendrix accepted, and his manager, Michael Jeffery, had only one condition—that Hendrix be the last to perform. The organizers expected an audience of 100,000, but over 500,000 young people showed up to the event, and the festival went down in history as the largest, most joyful musical gathering ever to take place. Because of delays, a lack of proper infrastructure and facilities, and heavy rain, Hendrix went onstage early in the morning on the concert's fourth day. By then, most of the crowd had already left. At 8:30 a.m., Hendrix went onstage and stated that he was tired of The Experience and that the larger band behind him would now be called Gypsy Sun and Rainbows. This was the beginning of one of the most memorable concerts of his career, and certainly one of the longest. The band played sixteen

THE WOODSTOCK GENERATION TRANSFORMED HENDRIX INTO A REVOLUTIONARY HERO

songs and an amazing rendition of the "Star Spangled Banner," which later became part of history thanks to Michael Wadleigh's famous documentary about the Woodstock Festival. Hendrix's interpretation was a veritable explosion of sounds—howls, groans, whistles, screams, shouts, blows, bangs, knocks, squeaks, scrapes and rumbles—an incredible version of the American national anthem that also featured the sound of bombs exploding (a reference to the Vietnam War). Even though no lyrics were sung, Hendrix's version of the national anthem became an important pacificist song. This not only helped put Hendrix's indelible stamp on the Woodstock Festival, it also became one of the defining moments of the 60s, which were about to end. "We washed and drank / in God's tears of joy / And for once… and for everyone… / The truth was not a mystery," wrote Hendrix in a poem about the event.

---

166 *Woodstock Music & Art Fair, held in Bethel, New York, in August of 1969. Behind Hendrix, bassist Billy Cox can be seen wearing a turban.*

168 A snapshot of the August 18, 1969 performance Jimi Hendrix gave at the Woodstock Music & Art Fair. Hendrix was the last artist to perform at the festival. His set was moved to the morning of the last day, but most of the spectators had already gone home by then. The show later became historic thanks in part to Jimi's amazing and frenzied rendition of the "Star Spangled Banner," which was included in the famous documentary film made about the festival.

169 One of the original posters advertising Woodstock. Because of all the chaos at the concert, some bands didn't end up performing, such as the Jeff Beck Group.

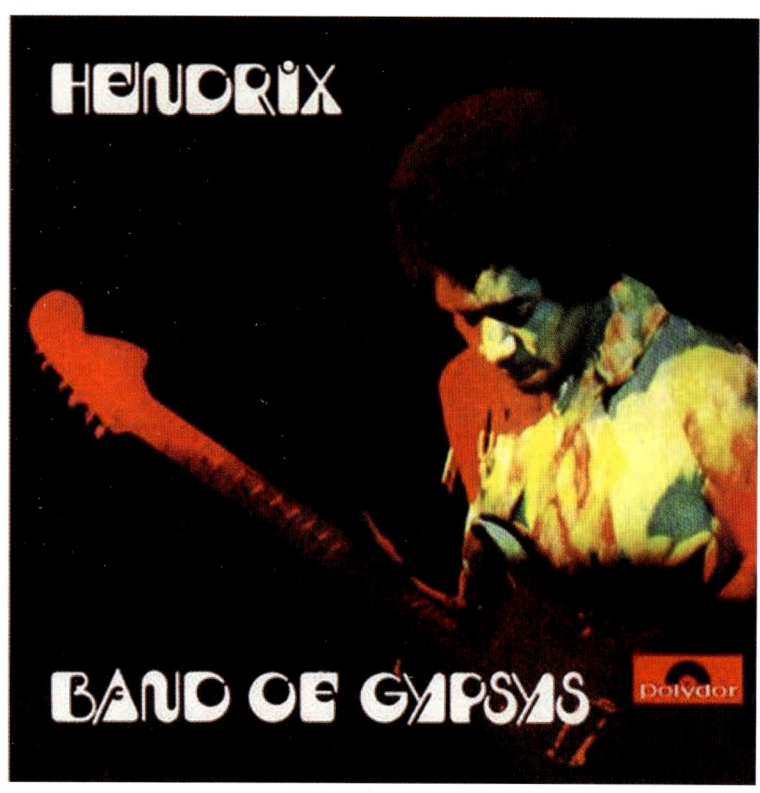

170 and 171 Two different covers of the Band of Gypsys album, which featured Billy Cox and Buddy Miles. The band was formed after the breakup of The Experience.

172 and 173 Another moment from Hendrix's performance at the 1967 Monterey Pop Festival.

That summer, Jimi couldn't make up his mind about anything, especially the lineup of his new band. The expanded band that had performed at Woodstock performed only another two concerts, one in Harlem and another in Greenwich Village. After a few studio recording sessions and the sessions recorded for a 1969 episode of the Dick Cavett Show, the band broke up. In December, Hendrix was acquitted of his drug possession charges in Canada. The menacing cloud of a prison sentence drifted away. Jimi immediately resumed making music at full speed. Because of a series of contractual problems with producer Ed Chaplin, Jimi was obligated to record a live album with a different band. With the help of Billy Cox and drummer Buddy Miles (who had played soul with Wilson Pickett and new rock with the Electric Flag band), Hendrix was able to prepare new material for a series of 1970 New Year concerts at the Fillmore East venue in New York. Many of the songs played during the concerts on the second day appeared on the album Band of Gypsys, which was produced by Hendrix himself. This was the only live album Hendrix released during his lifetime. The band produced a number of songs that didn't wind up on the album, including "Stepping Stone." This song and other tracks and recorded rehearsals were meant to serve as a new musical foundation that Hendrix hoped to build upon. But he wasn't sure if he was satisfied with the new lineup. He met many other musicians, including Miles Davis (according to Hendrix lore, the two played together on one occasion, privately, in a room inside Jimi's house), and spent many days reworking this new material, trying out different approaches and even inviting other musicians to rerecord parts for different instruments. Then, all of a sudden, Hendrix reached the conclusion that he wanted to resume his collaboration with The Experience. In mid-January of 1970, Mitch Mitchell and Noel Redding flew to New York to sign a contract for another Experience band tour with Hendrix. Jimi played with his Band of Gypsys one last time, at Madison Square Garden in New York on January 28, 1970 to benefit a protest organized by the Vietnam War Moratorium Committee.

HENDRIX RECORDED A LIVE ALBUM WITH THE BAND OF GYPSYS. THEIR LAST CONCERT WAS IN NEW YORK IN JANUARY OF 1970

One week later, in early February, the Jimi Hendrix Experience band was formed once again, at least on paper. But in reality, Jimi planned to replace Redding with Billy Cox.

A NEW DECADE HAD BEGUN.
THE 1970S SEEMED
full of promise and hope

During the next four months, Jimi concentrated on preparing songs for his next LP. He recorded in the studio during the week and played live shows on the weekends. At the same time, together with his friend Eddie Kramer, the sound engineer for all his albums, Jimi continued his work on the establishment of Electric Lady Studios in New York, spending most of his earnings on the project.

Creating the "perfect" recording studio had been one of Hendrix's dreams for a number of years. In fact, he had begun thinking about the idea in 1968, when he had bought the Generation Club in Greenwich Village. Michael Jeffery felt that the nightclub could be reopened, while Jimi thought the space would make for an ideal recording studio. After the *Electric Ladyland* sessions, he developed a strong interest in new recording techniques and wanted to experiment with them as much as possible. He wanted a place where he could avoid huge expenses and, more importantly, record whenever he felt like it, without having to submit to predetermined schedules. Jimi explained his project in detail to John Storyk, who designed the studio according to Jimi's specifications. Hendrix played in his new studio for the first time on June 15, 1970, in a session with Steve Winwood and Chris Wood from the band Traffic. The following day saw the first sessions for his new album, while Storyk continued to prepare the studio. It was officially opened on August 27, 1970. The next evening, Hendrix was in England with Mitch Mitchell and Billy Cox. They were playing the Isle of Wight Festival. The previous April, Cox, Mitchell, and Hendrix had gone on a 30-concert cross-country tour in the United States that Jeffery had insisted they undertake. The purpose was to enhance Hendrix's image and earn enough money to pay for the loan from Warner Brothers that was used to purchase the Generation Club and convert it into Electric Lady Studios. While on tour, the band played all the hits from The Experience's previous albums and many new songs. The trio was at the peak of its newfound power. During that tour, which ended on August 1, 1970, Hendrix gave some of his greatest and most memorable performances. But the same did not hold true for the second part of the tour, which took place in Europe. To begin with, Hendrix wasn't interested in playing those concerts. He wanted to return to his new studio to work on his new album. The European concerts were reportedly

Jimi opens Electric Lady Studios and begins work on a new album

somewhat lackluster. The band was worn out, and Hendrix had again ramped up his drug use, often spiraling out of control. To top it all off, some of the concerts had been sloppily organized, such as Aarus and Fehmarn. On September 6, the trio played for the last time. Hendrix went to London and reconnected with a woman he had met months earlier, German figure skater Monika Dannemann. He took a room at the Cumberland Hotel and spent time with old friends. He spoke with Chas Chandler and Eric Burdon and told them he wanted a new manager and that he was ready to make new music. His last live performance was with Burdon on September 16, at Ronnie Scott's Jazz Club. The two had a jam session with Burdon's band, War.

175 A photograph taken during Jimi's performance at the Isle of Wight in 1970. The festival marked the end of Hendrix's brief but brilliant career.

176 and 176–177 Jimi Hendrix onstage during the Love & Peace Festival, which was held on the island of Fehmarn in Germany on September 6, 1970. Twelve days later, Hendrix died in London.

On September 18, 1970, Hendrix spent the evening at a party. Monika Dannemann arrived and brought Hendrix back to her apartment in the basement of the Samarkand Hotel, at 22 Lansdowne Crescent, in the neighborhood of Notting Hill. The full circumstances of Hendrix's death are still unclear. Dannemann first stated that Hendrix went to bed as usual and that she had been unaware that he had swallowed several of her Vesparax sleeping pills (the normal dosage was half a pill). She didn't realize the condition Jimi was in until nine in the morning, when she saw he wasn't responsive. Panic-stricken, she called Eric Burdon and then an ambulance. When the doctors arrived, Hendrix was already dead, having suffocated on his own vomit. For years, Dannemann claimed that Hendrix had still been alive when the ambulance arrived a little after 11 a.m. and that she had followed him to the hospital in the ambulance, but this statement was denied by the numerous medical personnel that had gone to help Hendrix that morning. Both the British police and physicians reported that no one was in the apartment when they arrived at 11:27 a.m. on September 18 and that Hendrix had been dead for several hours.

London witnessed the arrival of a young, unknown American guitarist. When it saw him last, he had become one of the greatest guitarist of all time.

178 *Monika Danneman being helped by a friend as she leaves the Samarkand Hotel in London, where Jimi Hendrix died on September 18, 1970.*

179 *A copy of Jimi Hendrix's death certificate, which is on display in a small Hendrix museum on Brook Street in London.*

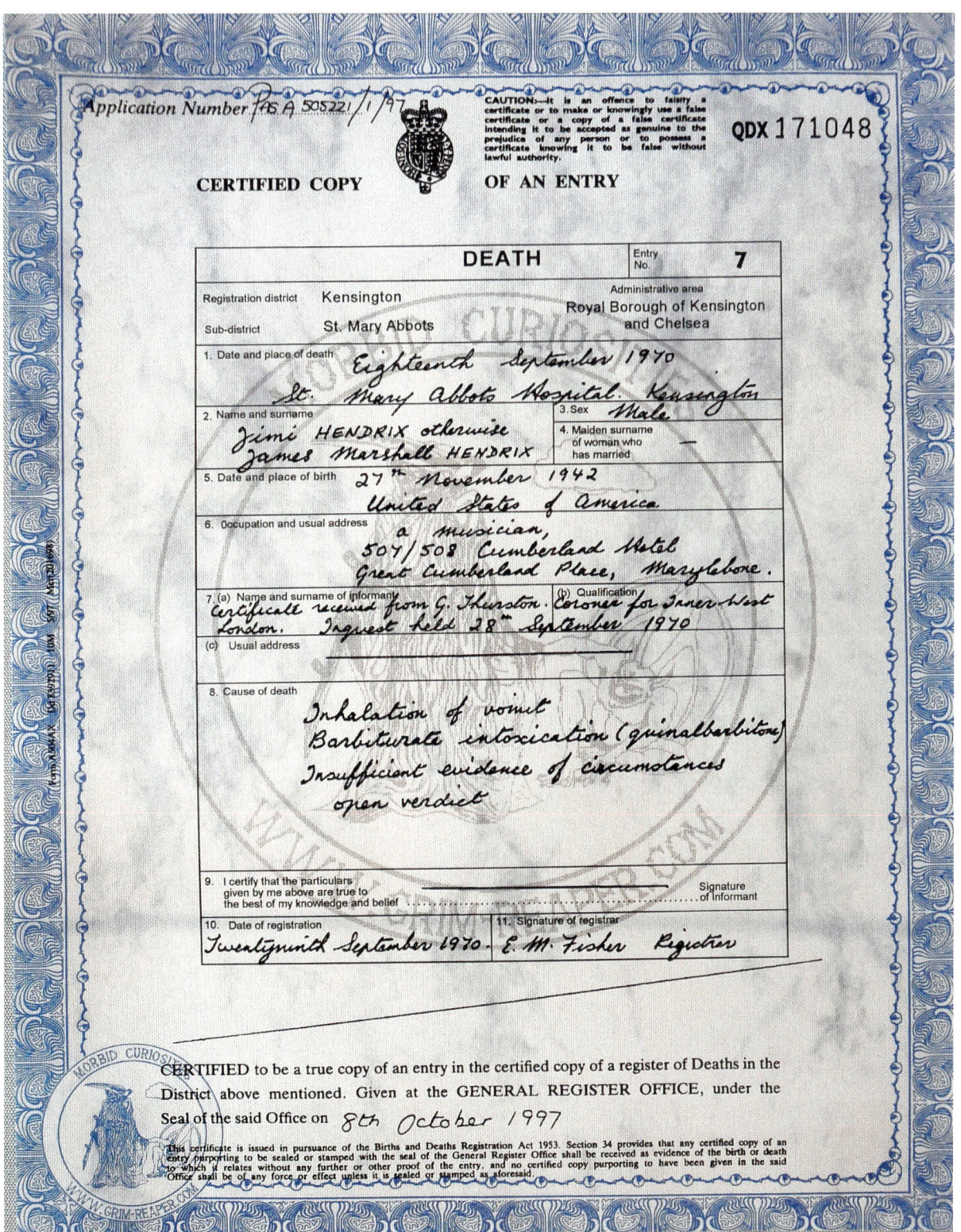

This was the final stage of a musical journey that had lasted barely four years. Yet these years were enough time for Hendrix to make three astonishing albums, record dozens of live concerts and demo tracks, and revolutionize what it meant to play the guitar. Besides the technical innovations he introduced, his performances evoked a sensation close to vertigo. He possessed instincts for improvisation matched only by jazz greats such as Charlie Parker and John Coltrane. And just like them, Jimi was always on the move toward the next big step in his musical evolution. But he ran out of time. In only four short years, he realized more than most successful musicians achieve in a lifetime, and he did it with only his guitar and the strength of his talent. Four rapid, relentless years dominated by an intense work ethic and a burning need to find the next party. The excesses of this lifestyle cost Jimi dearly in the end, but perhaps they were an inseparable part of his powerful personality.

HIS ROCK ADVENTURE LASTED ONLY FOUR EXTREMELY INTENSE YEARS, BUT WE'RE THANKFUL FOR WHAT WE HAVE

180 Jimi Hendrix's funeral service in Seattle, Washington. The funeral took place on October 1, 1970. His relatives and childhood friends can be seen following the coffin.

181 Leon, Jimi Hendrix's brother, can be seen here holding flowers. He is hugged by his girlfriend after Jimi has just been buried in Greenwood Memorial Park in Renton, Washington.

"The moment I feel that I don't have anything more to give musically, that's when I won't be found on this planet," Hendrix said once during an interview. "Unless I have a wife and children. Because if I don't have anything to communicate through my music, then there is nothing for me to live for. I'm not sure I will live to be 28 years old, but then again, so many beautiful things have happened to me in the last three years. The world owes me nothing.

"When people fear death, it's a complete case of insecurity. Your body is only a physical vehicle to carry you from one place to another without getting into a lot of trouble. . . . The idea is to get your own self together, see if you can get ready for the next world, because there is one. Hope you can dig it. . . . I tell you, when I die I'm going to have a jam session. I want people to go wild and freak out. And knowing me, I'll probably get busted at my own funeral. The music will be played loud and it will be our music. I won't have Beatles songs, but I'll have a few of Eddie Cochran's things and a whole lot of blues. Roland Kirk will be there, and I'll try and get Miles Davis along if he feels like making it. For that it's almost worth dying. . . . When I die, just keep on playing the records."

> "Roland Kirk will be there, and I'll go and get Miles Davis along if he feels like making it. For that it's almost worth dying."

183 *The great jazz trumpeter and composer Miles Davis arriving with his wife Betty Mabry (at left) and a friend to Jimi Hendrix's funeral, which was held on October 1, 1970 in Seattle.*

1970

7 INTERVIEWS

MEMORIES, EMOTIONS, AND THOUGHTS FROM THOSE WHO KNEW HIM

BILLY COX

Who knows what the great Jimi Hendrix would have played today? He who revolutionized the use and lexicon of the guitar, who proposed to the world some of the most overwhelming guitar solos imaginable, who took his instrument to the apex of creativity and transformed it into the symbol of a generation and an era.

"He would have played the music of the angels, music than no one has ever heard," says bassist Billy Cox, who was close to Hendrix as both a friend and a fellow musician. In fact, Cox was one of Jimi's oldest friends. They met while serving in the US Army and, as Cox has stated, "gelled from the very beginning" and began to play together. Today he is the only surviving member of Hendrix's bands (The Jimi Hendrix Experience, Band of Gypsys, and Gypsy Sun and Rainbows) and, as he loves to say, he carries the torch and continues to testify to the greatness, creativity, and sheer power of the best electric guitarist of all time: "We were friends and we lived music. But he was ahead of everyone else, he had arrived on this earth from another galaxy.

Billy Cox was the musician closest to Hendrix

Nowadays it's hard to understand how creative, innovative, and unique Jimi was. But at that time, it wasn't hard, and playing with him was an extraordinary experience."

Like at Woodstock, one of the last times you played together.

"It was the first concert I did with Jimi from the time he had become famous and I had never played in front of such a huge crowd. I remember when we arrived and saw the audience, Mitch Mitchell and I almost freaked out. Jimi on the other hand remained calm and said that we would be able to take great energy from the crowd, which would help us. He was right. On the Woodstock stage, he not only surprised the spectators but us as well. We had rehearsed a repertoire and we played that repertoire. . . .When he began to play the notes of the 'Star Spangled Banner,' the American anthem, we were surprised and puzzled. We had never rehearsed that. And yet this incredible performance became historic."

How did you work with Hendrix?

"A lot was based on the jams. We would improvise and I would follow his lead. The bass parts were written across a riff, which Jimi created. We improvised, found a riff that made sense, and connected the parts until it was all done. We were able to finish a song in three or four sessions. At other times, Jimi would arrive in the studio with a more complete idea, so we worked on finding the right sound with the bass in order not to lose the initial inspiration. He and I always improvised a lot together, from the time we were youngsters. We were on the same special wavelength, he knew what I was about to do and I knew what he was going to do. I think that talent helped us. We would start off from a simple blues base or some classic like 'Johnny B. Goode,' and anything could happen. We were on that same special wavelength, which was not only technical or musical—it was a question of spirit, of understanding. Neither of us had such a big ego as to want to neutralize the other. In fact, we each looked for support from the other so we could do new, different, more adventurous things. And then, my role was to support Jimi; I wasn't the soloist, and it was a role I really liked."

Jimi also played bass and often used his guitar like a bass.

"Yes, he was a good bassist. In fact, on some albums he would play the bass parts directly. The part I think is most beautiful is the one in 'All Along the Watchtower.'"

What was he like?

"He was a good person, respectable, kind, generous, and naive at times. But passionate, full of energy, enthusiastic. And he wasn't the kind of person who liked excess. As far as I know he never had a drug problem, he wasn't one of those who went around stoned all day long or who was always looking for drugs. Certainly none of us was an angel, but it's equally certain that he was not an addict. The only addiction he had was music; he was amazingly concentrated, attentive, and creative where music was concerned."

You met while doing military service.

"Yes, we were in the army together at Fort Campbell, Kentucky. That's where I heard him play the first time. I was returning to the barracks with another soldier when it began to rain, so we took shelter under the roof of a barrack. There was an open window and out of it came the sound of a guitar. I was curious and looked inside. There was a lanky kid who was playing alone. I went in and introduced myself, said that I also loved music and played the bass. We got along right off and remained friends until the end."

Who is Hendrix's successor today?

"Well, I don't think there is any electric guitarist who can ignore his work, what he did. Everyone, in some way or another has been influenced by him. But there have been no successors, and we'll never see anyone else like him on the stage."

The sound of Cox's bass marks the final phase of Hendrix's music and makes us wonder what he might have become had he lived longer.

188-189 *The bassist Billy Cox performing at the Fox Theater in Atlanta, Georgia on February 27, 2016. The concert was dedicated to Jimi Hendrix and his music.*

LEON HENDRIX

Leon Hendrix is over 70, but he is still known as Jimi Hendrix's "little brother."

"I don't mind," he says. "He was a real big brother; he helped me and protected me. He did what every big brother knows how to do. He was my hero and I had a lot of fun with him."

Leon Hendrix is a musician and likes to play his brother's music.

"Yes, I play my own stuff, but I love to play Jimi's songs, too. It's thrilling. To this day his music is really very contemporary."

Are there songs you're particularly attached to?

"I really love 'Angel,' obviously, because it's a song that Jimi wrote thinking about our mother, who died when we were both very young."

You had a complicated childhood.

Jimi and Leon always had each other. Leon continues to play his brother's songs to help remember him

"Yes, but to tell the truth, it wasn't all that bad. Certainly our father Al had drinking problems, but he always did his best to make sure we were all right. Our mother abandoned us when we were still very young, but we had a large family and many other persons liked us. Jimi and I were always together. He took care of me and we had fun. My father would go to work and Jimi was my babysitter; I followed him wherever he went. So I recall everything of that period, I remember when he began to play the guitar, his first concerts. . . . I would go backstage to see what he was doing. I was only twelve."

Did Jimi want to become a great guitarist?

"I don't know how aware he was of his gifts when he was a kid. He was very passionate about music and worked on learning to play the guitar with infinite energy. And then he knew he wanted this to become his work, he wanted to have a life of music and nothing else. He wasn't particularly interested in fame or money; he was already happy, really happy when he was in New York and played in clubs. He had a car, a girlfriend, some money to get along. . . . Music was the only thing he wanted, always new music."

Was he really timid?

"He was as extroverted onstage as he was timid once he got off the stage. In reality he was rather introverted, but very good and kind. He expressed his feelings through music, not words. You could see what he was going through in his mind by looking at his eyes while he was playing. I was just the opposite, a rowdy extrovert, over the top. I would run all around while he would sit down to think, imagine, dream."

After his stint in the army, you and he had less contact. Was this because Jimi had begun traveling and gigging here and there?

"Yes, we began to see him less, he never came home. But he always wrote to us, and it was great for me to know that he was playing with anyone, even with great stars. And he never wanted to stay put or be idle. He continuously changed bands, always had new experiences, and worked a hell of a lot. He was the best guitarist around, so they were always asking him to play. But he was not happy, he wanted different things, always."

Was his career as a soloist like that too?

"Certainly. The disbanding of The Experience was due to this. He didn't want to always repeat the same things, he was always searching for something new, different musicians he could play with, different experiences. He was an explorer of music and simply couldn't stay still. He wanted to evolve together with his music."

At a certain point, you got together again.

"Yes, but that story is complicated . . . . I was in the army and found out on the radio that Jimi was about to give a concert in a place near my barracks, so I went to the concert and then went to meet him at the airport. Jimi told me to follow him, to go with him on tour, and I agreed. But I was in the army, so at the end of the tour I ended up in prison as a deserter. But that wasn't my intention. Jimi and my father helped me, and the matter was resolved."

Your brother's death was quite a blow.

"I was in prison because of the tour. We said goodbye before they arrested me. He wanted to go to the Hawaiian Islands, so we made a date to see one another in New York. I returned to Seattle, and the military police took me away, and a few days later Jimi sent me money to organize my defense. I was in prison at Monroe, Washington, and they sent for me and told me there was a phone call for me. When a call of that kind arrives in prison, it means either that you're about to be released or that someone has died, and I knew very well that I was not due to leave prison for another six months. I went from my cell to the office in total silence. It was my father on the phone; he told me about it and we both cried."

What does it mean for you today to take your brother's music around the world?

"It's all I can do. As for the rest, things have gone differently. But I don't complain, I have a good job. . . ."

192 Leon Hendrix, Jimi Hendrix's younger brother, in a photograph taken on September 28, 2015. Today he is a musician and producer.

193 Leon Hendrix during a concert at the legendary Whisky a Go Go club in Los Angeles, California.

EDDIE KRAMER

Eddie Kramer was 25 when he first met Jimi Hendrix and began working as a sound engineer on his tracks. He had a hand in preparing all of Hendrix's albums and was his technical and creative partner. To this day, when we listen to those albums, we grasp Kramer's amazing creative capacity. But the true "experience" is listening to *Electric Ladyland* in 5.1 surround sound, a version of the album that Eddie Kramer made in 2019.

"This is a dream come true," Kramer says. "I've had many other occasions to work on Hendrix's repertory, it was so rich in live recordings and outtakes that remastering it was both easy and obvious. But the challenge to use high-resolution audio and surround on something I myself did so many years ago is truly unbelievable."

From an emotional standpoint as well?

"Especially. In transferring the twelve tracks of the recordings to present-day standards, I heard mind-boggling things—Jimi's voice, my comments, our joking with the band—something beautiful and frightening at the same time, like being literally transported back in time."

Hendrix was lucky to have Kramer as his studio sidekick during his recording years

An important period, because a new life was beginning for both you and Hendrix.

"Yes, it's true. A new life began for us both. I had followed Jimi to the United States and I had had an offer from Record Plant Studios. For Jimi this was fantastic. He arrived from London, where he recorded on four tracks, as he had done with his first two albums, while Record Plant had twelve tracks, and this made him go crazy, because he felt he could put so many more things in his music."

And everything changed in a few weeks.

"It was a philosophical change, on the one hand, and one of attitude. Everything shifted in his brain, and this led him to do only what he felt was right. We were fortunate, since the record companies at that time weren't afraid of innovation and they appreciated changes. And above all, he was an enormously popular artist, so they let him decide what to do."

What was the key element in *Electric Ladyland*?

"The perfect balance between experimentation and entertainment, between enjoyment and surprise."

And what was it like to work with him?

"Try to imagine what it was like in New York, between 8th Ave and 46th St, when 1968 was in full swing. This was where his favorite club, The Scene, was, where he often went to play. We recorded for most of the day, then he would leave and go to jam in the club. The English musical revolution had brought a great many artists to New York, and Jimi met them and played with them every evening. He understood who was cool and who wasn't, and if he really liked someone, he would take him or her to the studio. He would leave the club with a group of 20 persons following him, arrive at Record Plant Studios with the guitar in his hand, and play. And we were all ready to follow him. And he would make recording after recording until he was really satisfied. This was how 'Voodoo Chile' was created."

Is there a song that you're especially fond of?

"'Little Wing,' without a doubt. I still cry when I listen to it. I remember Jimi playing this song in front of me and my being moved."

So, what's it like to do the remastering now?

"It's hard and exciting, because the technology at that time was light-years away from what we have today. Now we move the music 360 degrees and mix with five plus one channels to recreate the effects that Hendrix wanted then, just as I believe he would want them today."

So he wasn't afraid at all?

"Jimi was never afraid of challenges. 'There's nothing I wouldn't do with music,' he would say. Well, I totally agree."

How was it that you began to work with Hendrix?

"It was in January of 1967. I had already recorded some singles, such as 'Hey Joe,' and everyone was talking about him, even greats such as Clapton and McCartney. Paul in particular appreciated his music. So much so that, when he found out they were organizing the Monterey Pop Festival, he phoned the organizers and told them that they simply had to include Jimi Hendrix in the program. And that phone call totally changed Jimi's career, because it allowed him to return to America and become known outside of England. Chas Chandler called and asked me to work on Jimi's first album, *Are You Experienced*. At that time, Jimi didn't have any original material, and Chas urged him to write songs, find new riffs, and put his ideas together.

So Jimi began to write, and from then on it was like a tsunami. He was not only a great guitarist, as everyone now acknowledges, obviously, but also a fine songwriter. When I began working with him in the studio, I wondered whether I would be able to record what he played, whether I could make him play on the album in the same way, or even better, than how he played live."

There's always been a part of the public that preferred Hendrix live and another part that liked his studio work. Which side are you on?

"Both. He was superb live as well as in the studio. I didn't work with him only in the studio, I recorded many live performances, some of which are matchless, for example the one at Woodstock.

196 *Sound engineer Eddie Kramer standing behind Jimi Hendrix in the control room of the studio on June 17, 1970.*

197 *Eddie Kramer in front of a photograph of Jimi Hendrix. This photo was taken during a Hendrix exhibition at the Proud Gallery in London.*

However, there's a different level in the studio; there's the same immediacy, but you can take your time trying out different solutions. I believe that it was in *Electric Ladyland* that Jimi succeeded in lending greater power and form to everything in his brain, experimenting and enjoying himself."

Do you remember your first meeting?

"Yes. We were at Olympic Studios. We had never seen each other before. We introduced ourselves and spoke very little at first. Jimi was rather timid. He sat in a corner of the studio and waited until everything was ready. Then he just waded right into his guitar, and what came out was nothing more or less than an explosion of sound. I asked myself what the devil I could do, how would I be able to work with that electrifying sound? So I did my job, manipulated the sliders. Then Jimi came into the control room and I had him listen to the result. He gave a big smile, said nothing, went back to the live room, and set about revving up the amplifiers and pedals; then he resumed playing, and I started up the recorders again. It was a sort of challenge. Each of us tried to do better every time, tried to do things that hadn't been done before or tried to make the sounds expand as far as the impossible. It was always like that, up to the end. And we had a great time trying to express and translate the things that Jimi felt inside himself, the ideas that came to him also in the middle of the night, in dreams. His mind was open to everything."

> "It was a sort of challenge. Each of us tried to do better every time, tried to do things that hadn't been done before. . . ."

What is it of Hendrix that you miss most?

"His capacity to view the world with eyes that were different from everyone else's eyes."

---

199 *From left to right: Jim Marron, Eddie Kramer, Mitch Mitchell, Jimi Hendrix, Billy Cox, and Noel Redding standing behind an unidentified pregnant woman in Jimi's Electric Lady Studios in New York (June 17, 1970).*

"WHEN I DIE, JUST KEEP PLAYING THE RECORDS"

Discography

STUDIO-RECORDED ALBUMS

ARE YOU EXPERIENCED
May 1967
Label: Track (612 001)
Foxey Lady
Manic Depression
Red House
Can You See Me
Love or Confusion
I Don't Live Today
May This Be Love
Fire
Third Stone From the Sun
Remeber
Are You Experienced

AXIS: BOLD AS LOVE
December 1967
Label: Track (613 003)
EXP
Up From the Skies
Spanish Castle Magic
Wait Until Tomorrow
Ain't No Telling
Little Wing
If 6 Was 9
You Got Me Floatin'
Castles Made Of Sand
She's So Fine
One Rainy Wish
Little Miss Lover
Bold as Love

ELECTRIC LADYLAND
October 1968
Label: Track (613 008/9)
...And the Gods Made Love
Have You Ever Been (To Electric Ladyland)
Crosstown Traffic
Voodoo Chile
Little Miss Strange
Long Hot Summer Night
Come On (Let the Good Times Roll)
Gypsy Eyes
Burning of the Midnight Lamp
Rainy Day, Dream Away
1983... (A Merman I Should Turn to Be)
Moon, Turn the Tides.... Gently Gently Away
Still Raining, Still Dreaming
House Burning Down
All Along the Watchtower
Voodoo Child (Slight Return)

ABUMS RECORDED LIVE

BAND OF GYPSYS
March 1970
Label: Capitol (STAO-472)
Who Knows
Machine Gun
Changes
Power To Love
Message Of Love
We Gotta Live Together

COLLECTIONS

SMASH HITS
April 1968
Label: Track (613004)
Purple Haze
Fire
The Wind Cries Mary
Can You See Me
Hey Joe
All Along the Watchtower
Stone Free
Crosstown Traffic
Manic Depression
Remember
Red House
Foxey Lady

201 A poster portraying Hendrix. It was designed by Martin Sharp in 1968.

202 Hendrix in a 1969 color lithograph by Gunther Kieser.

Posthumous Discography

STUDIO ALBUMS

CRY OF LOVE
March 1971
Label: Reprise (MS 2034)

RAINBOW BRIDGE
October 1971
Label: Reprise (MS 2040)

WAR HEROES
October 1972
Label: Polydor (2302 020)

LOOSE ENDS
February 1974
Label: Polydor (2310 301)

CRASH LANDING
March 1975
Label: Reprise (MS 2204)

MIDNIGHT LIGHTNING
November 1975
Label: Reprise (MS 2229)

NINE TO THE UNIVERSE
March 1980
Label: Reprise (HS 2299)

FIRST RAYS OF THE NEW RISING SUN
April 1997
Label: MCA (#11599)

SOUTH SATURN DELTA
October 1997
Label: MCA (#11684)

VALLEYS OF NEPTUNE
March 2010
Label: Sony Legacy (88697640591)

PEOPLE, HELL & ANGELS
March 2013
Label: Sony Legacy (88759947289)

BOTH SIDES OF THE SKY
March 2018
Label: Sony Legacy (95347234854)

ALBUMS RECORDED LIVE

EXPERIENCE
August 1971
Label: Ember (5057)

ISLE OF WIGHT
November 1971
Label: Polydor (2302 016)

HENDRIX IN THE WEST
February 1972
Label: Reprise (MS 2049)

MORE EXPERIENCE
March 1972
Label: Ember (NR 5061)

WOKE UP THIS MORNING AND FOUND MYSELF DEAD
August 1980
Label: Red Lightnin' Records (#RL CD 0068)

THE JIMI HENDRIX CONCERTS
August 1982
Label: Reprise (#2306)

JIMI PLAYS MONTEREY
February 1986
Label: Reprise (#25358)

JOHNNY B. GOODE
June 1986
Label: Capitol (MLP 15022)

BAND OF GYPSYS 2
October 1986
Label: Capitol (SJ 12416)

LIVE AT WINTERLAND
May 1987
Label: Rykodisc (RCD #0038)

RADIO ONE
November 1988
Label: Ryko Analogue (#0078)

LIVE AT THE ISLE OF WIGHT
June 1991
Label: Polydor (847 236-2)

BLEEDING HEART
May 1994
Label: Castle (MACCD 190)

WOODSTOCK
August 1994
Label: MCA (#11603)

LIVE AT THE OAKLAND COLISEUM
February 1998
Label: MCA (#11987)

BBC SESSIONS
June 1998
Label: MCA (#11742)

LIVE AT THE FILLMORE EAST
February 1999
Label: MCA (#11931)

LIVE AT WOODSTOCK
July 1999
Label: MCA (#11987)

LIVE AT CLARK UNIVERSITY
July 1999
Label: MCA (#11987)

LIVE IN OTTAWA
March 2001
Label: MCA (#11987)

BLUE WILD ANGEL: LIVE AT THE ISLE OF WIGHT
November 2002
Label: MCA (#113 087)

PARIS 1967/SAN FRANCISCO 1968
April 2003
Label: MCA (#11987)

LIVE AT BERKELEY
September 2003
Label: MCA (#B0001102)

LIVE AT THE ISLE OF FEHMARN
December 2005
Label: MCA (#B0001102)

LIVE AT MONTEREY
October 2007
Label: Geffen (#B0009845)

LIVE IN PARIS & OTTAWA 1968
September 2008
Label: MCA (#11986)

LIVE AT WORBUN
July 2009
Label: MCA (#11987)

WINTERLAND
13 September 2011
Label: Sony (#B0009845)

LIVE IN COLOGNE
October 2012
Label: MCA (#11988)

MIAMI POP FESTIVAL
November 2013
Label: Sony (#B00F031X62)

FREEDOM: ATLANTA POP FESTIVAL
August 2015
Label: Sony Legacy (#B0047824X9)

MACHINE GUN: THE FILLMORE EAST FIRST SHOW
September 2016
Label: Sony Legacy (#B00W46764)

SONGS FOR GROOVY CHILDREN
November 2019
Label: Sony Legacy (#B07Y9BWCT1)

AUTHOR

ERNESTO ASSANTE began working as a journalist in 1977. During a career spanning over 30 years, he has contributed to many Italian and foreign weeklies and monthlies including *Epoca*, *L'Espresso*, and *Rolling Stone*. He created and oversaw supplements such as "Musica," "Computer Valley," and "Computer, Internet, e Altro" for the Italian daily *La Repubblica*. Assante has also written books on music criticism, often in collaboration with his colleague, Gino Castaldo. Since 2005, Assante and Castaldo have hosted "Lessons in Rock: Journey to the Center of Music," a series of multimedia presentations that delve into the history and legendary figures of rock music. From 2003 to 2009, Assante taught at Sapienza University in Rome. His classes included Theory and Technique of New Media and Analysis of Musical Languages. He has written several books for White Star Publishers.

Photo Credits

Page 5: David Montgomery/Getty Images
Page 7: Mira/Alamy Stock Photo
Pages 8-9: Bruce Fleming/Getty Images
Pages 10-11: Framed Art/Alamy Stock Photo
Page 13: Christopher Smith/123RF
Page 17: Apic/Getty Images
Page 25: Christopher Smith/123RF
Page 28: Don Paulsen/Michael Ochs Archives/Getty Images
Page 29: Gilles Petard/Redferns/Getty Images
Page 31: Cyrus Andrews/Michael Ochs archives/Getty Images
Page 32: Trinity Mirror/Mirrorpix/Alamy Stock Photo
Pages 34-35: Jan Olofsson/Redferns/Getty Images
Page 36: K & K Ulf Kruger OHG/Redferns/Getty Images
Page 37: Michael Ochs Archives/Getty Images
Pages 38-39: Pictorial Press Ltd/Alamy Stock Photo
Pages 40-41: James Andanson/Sygma/Getty Images
Page 41: Fiona Adams/Redferns/Getty Images
Page 42: Pictorial Press Ltd/Alamy Stock Photo
Page 43: Pictorial Press Ltd/Alamy Stock Photo
Pages 44-45: Hulton Archive/Getty Images
Page 47: Christopher Smith/123RF
Page 50: Private Collection/ Photo © Christie's Images/Bridgeman Images
Page 51: Pictorial Press Ltd/Alamy Stock Photo
Page 52: Lebrecht Music Arts/Bridgeman Images
Page 54: Spaarnestad Photo/Bridgeman Images
Page 55: Spaarnestad Photo/Bridgeman Images
Page 57: Michael Ochs Archives/Getty Images
Page 58: private collection
Page 59: private collection
Page 60: Framed Art/Alamy Stock Photo
Page 61: GAB Archive/Redferns/Getty Images
Page 62: Daily Mirror/Mirrorpix/Getty Images
Page 63: Mirrorpix
Page 64: © Mirrorpix/Bridgeman Images
Page 65: Mirrorpix
Pages 66-67: K & K Ulf Kruger OHG/Redferns/Getty Images
Page 67: K & K Ulf Kruger OHG/Redferns/Getty Images
Page 69: John D. Kisch/Separate Cinema Archive/Getty Images
Page 70: Michael Ochs Archives/Getty Images

Page 71: Michael Ochs Archives/Getty Images
Page 73: Ed Caraeff/Getty Images
Pages 74-75: Gareth Cattermole/Getty Images
Pages 76-77: Ivan Keeman/Redferns/Getty Images
Page 78: Michael Putland/Getty Images
Page 79: Bridgeman Images
Page 80: Monitor Picture Library/Photoshot/Getty Images
Page 81: Photoshot /Getty Images
Pages 82-83: © united archives/Leemage/United Archives GmbH/Bridgeman Images
Page 84: Pictorial Press Ltd/Alamy Stock Photo
Page 85: Records/Alamy Stock Photo
Page 86: Ed Caraeff/Getty Images
Page 87: Ed Caraeff/Getty Images
Page 88: Trinity Mirror/Mirrorpix/Alamy Stock Photo
Page 89: Mirrorpix
Page 90: Jimi Hendrix/Bridgeman Images
Page 91: Private Collection/ Photo © Christie's Images/Bridgeman Images
Pages 92-93: Pictorial Press Ltd/Alamy Stock Photo
Pages 94-95: Pictorial Press Ltd/Alamy Stock Photo
Page 95: Pictorial Press Ltd/Alamy Stock Photo
Pages 96-97: Michael Ochs Archives/Getty Images
Page 98: David Redfern/Redferns/Getty Images
Page 100: The Advertising Archives/Alamy Stock Photo
Page 101: The Advertising Archives/Alamy Stock Photo
Page 102: King Collection/Photoshot/Getty Images
Page 104: Trinity Mirror/Mirrorpix/Alamy Stock Photo
Page 106: CBW/Alamy Stock Photo
Page 107 center: CBW/Alamy Stock Photo
Page 107 bottom: Records/Alamy Stock Photo
Page 108: David Redfern/Redferns/Getty Images
Page 110: David Redfern/Redferns/Getty Images
Page 113: © Hulton-Deutsch Collection/CORBIS/Getty Images
Page 114: Fred W. McDarrah/Getty Images
Page 117: Christopher Smith/123RF
Page 120: Trinity Mirror/Mirrorpix/Alamy Stock Photo
Page 121: Trinity Mirror/Mirrorpix/Alamy Stock Photo
Pages 122-123: Eric Harlow/Mirrorpix/Getty Images
Page 123: Trinity Mirror/Mirrorpix/Alamy Stock Photo
Page 125: Fred W. McDarrah/Getty Images
Page 127: Keyston Press/Alamy Stock Photo
Page 129: Christopher Smith/123RF
Pages 132-133: Baron Wolman/Getty Images
Page 135: Larry Hulst/Michael Ochs Archives/Getty Images
Page 137: Michael Ochs Archives/Getty Images
Pages 138-139: Michael Ochs Archives/Getty Images
Pages 140-141: Bruce Fleming/Getty Images
Pages 142-143: WENN Rights Ltd/Alamy Stock Photo
Pages 144-145: Pictorial Press Ltd/Alamy Stock Photo
Page 146: MediaPunch Inc./Alamy Stock Photo
Page 147: MediaPunch Inc./Alamy Stock Photo
Page 148: © Hulton-Deutsch Collection/CORBIS/Getty Images
Page 149: PA Images/Getty Images
Page 150 left: Jorgen Angel/Redferns/Getty Images
Page 150 right: Jorgen Angel/Redferns/Getty Images
Page 151: Jan Persson/Redferns/Getty Images
Page 152: Baron Wolman/Getty Images
Page 153: Doug McKenzie/Getty Images
Page 154: Nigel Osbourne/Redferns/Getty Images
Page 155: Tom Copi/Michael Ochs Archives/Getty Images
Page 156: Clive Gee-PA Images/Getty Images
Page 157 left: Nigel Osbourne/Redferns/Getty Images
Page 157 right: Photo © Christie's Images/Bridgeman Images
Pages 158-159: Jan Persson/Redferns/Getty Images
Page 161: Christopher Smith/123RF
Page 164: Donaldson Collection/Michael Ochs Archives/Getty Images
Page 166: Henry Diltz/Corbis/Getty Images
Page 168: MediaPunch Inc./Alamy Stock Photo
Page 169: Interfoto/Alamy Stock Photo/IPA
Page 170: private collection
Page 171: private collection
Page 172: Bruce Fleming/Getty Images
Page 175: David Redfern/Redferns/Getty Images
Page 176: Michael Ochs Archives/Getty Images
Pages 176-177: Peter Timm/ullstein bild/Getty Images
Page 178: Trinity Mirror/Mirrorpix/Alamy Stock Photo
Page 179: Ian Nicholson/PA Images/Getty Images
Page 180: Michael Ochs Archives/Getty Images
Page 181: Bettmann/Getty Images
Page 183: Bob Peterson/The LIFE Images Collection/Getty Images
Page 185: Christopher Smith/123RF
Pages 188-189: Chris McKay/Getty Images
Page 192: ZUMA Press Inc./Alamy Stock Photo
Page 193: ZUMA Press Inc./Alamy Stock Photo
Page 196: Fred W.McDarrah/Getty Images
Page 197: ukartpics/Alamy Stock Photo
Page 199: Fred W.McDarrah/Getty Images
Page 201: Christie's Images, London/Scala, Firenze
Page 202: Bridgeman Images

Project Editor

Valeria Manferto De Fabianis

Graphic Designer

Paola Piacco

WS White Star Publishers® is a registered trademark property of White Star s.r.l.

© 2020 White Star s.r.l.
Piazzale Luigi Cadorna, 6
20123 Milan, Italy
www.whitestar.it

Translation: Richard Pierce - Editing: Leo Costigan

All rights reserved. No part of this publication may be reproduced, stored in a retrieval system, or transmitted in any form or by any means, including electronic, mechanical, photocopying, recording, or otherwise, without written permission from the publisher.

ISBN 978-88-544-1663-5
1 2 3 4 5 6   24 23 22 21 20

Printed in Serbia